THE UTTER RELIEF
OF HOLINESS

*How God's Goodness Frees Us
from Everything that Plagues Us*

JOHN ELDREDGE

HODDER &
STOUGHTON

CONTENTS

PART I

THE SURPRISE OF HOLINESS

May God himself, the God of peace, sanctify you through and through. May your whole spirit, soul and body be kept blameless at the coming of our Lord Jesus Christ. The one who calls you is faithful and he will do it.

1 Thessalonians 5:23–24

CHAPTER ONE

AN UTTER RELIEF

One of the strangest quirks of our life here on this planet is the fact that the one face we hardly ever see is the one closest to us: our own. As we move about in the world every day, our face is always right before us and always just beyond us. Somebody could write a fairy tale about that. It would be an allegory for how rarely we see ourselves, who we truly are, the good and the bad. But in unexpected moments we get a sideways glance, as when passing by a plateglass window downtown, and most of the time we don't like much what we see.

Notice how we are in elevators: No one makes eye contact. No one wants to acknowledge that we are seeing and being seen. In a moment of forced intimacy, almost claustrophobic intimacy, we pretend we aren't even there. The reason? Most times we just don't know what to do with what we see. About ourselves, I mean.

It doesn't take a Nobel Prize winner to know that something dreadful has happened to the human race. So we stare at the ceiling or our shoes; we watch the numbers report the passing floors; we hide. This is how most of us approach our entire lives—we hide what we can, work on what we feel is redeemable, and despise the rest.

There is a better way.

The first chapter of Khaled Hosseini's novel *Kite Runner* begins with an arresting sentence: "I became what I am today at the age of twelve, on a frigid overcast day in the winter of 1975." It is the beginning of a confession. He continues:

> I remember the precise moment, crouching behind a crumbling mud wall, peeking into the alley near the frozen creek. That was a long time ago, but it's wrong what they say about the past, I've learned, about how you can bury it. Because the past claws its way out. Looking back now, I realize I have been peeking into that deserted alley for the last twenty-six years.
>
> One day last summer, my friend Rahim Khan called from Pakistan. He asked me to come see him. Standing in the kitchen with the receiver to my ear, I knew it wasn't just Rahim Khan on the line. It was my past of unatoned sins.

Oh, my. What if your past of unatoned sins called you on the phone one day? How would you feel? What would you say?

> I sat on a park bench near a willow tree. I thought about something Rahim Khan said just before he hung up, almost as an afterthought. *There is a way to be good again.* I looked up at those twin kites. I thought about Hassan. Thought about Baba. Ali. Kabul. I thought of the life I had lived until the winter of 1975 came along and changed everything. And made me what I am today.

Every one of us could write a similar confession. That is, if we saw things clearly, we, too, could say, "This is what I am today; this is what has made me what I am today."

My favorite line in the entire novel is this one: "There is a way to be good again."

Whether you are aware of it or not, you crave goodness. (Something caused you to pick up a book with the word *holiness* in the title!) In the depths of your being, you ache for goodness; we all do. Our souls long for a sense of wholeness, and goodness is essential for wholeness. We are made for goodness like we are made to breathe, like we are made to love. Goodness is the strength of our condition. Friends, you are going to need a deep and profound goodness for all that is coming at you like a freight train. And there is a way to be good again. It comes to us from such a surprising direction—as almost all of the answers to our deepest needs do—that we'd best begin with a question: What is Christianity supposed to *do* to a person?

How God Restores Human Beings

We exercise because we want to grow stronger; we take vitamins in the hope of being healthy; we attend language classes expecting to learn a new language. We travel for adventure; we work in the hope of prospering; we love partly in the hope of being loved. So why Christianity? What is the *effect* Christianity is intended to have upon a person who becomes a Christian, seeks to live as a Christian?

The way you answer that question is mighty important. Your beliefs about this will shape your convictions about nearly everything else. It will shape your understanding of the purpose of the Gospel; it will shape your understanding of what you believe God is up to in a person's life. The way you answer this one question will shape your thoughts about church and community, service and justice, prayer and worship. It is currently shaping the way you interpret your experiences and your beliefs about your relationship with God.

What is Christianity supposed to *do* to a person?

How blessed is God! And what a blessing he is! He's the Father of our Master, Jesus Christ, and takes us to the high places of blessing in him. Long before he laid down earth's foundations, he had us in mind, had settled on us as the focus of his love, to be made whole and holy by his love. Long, long ago he decided to adopt us into his family through Jesus Christ. (What pleasure he took in planning this!) He wanted us to enter into the celebration of his lavish gift-giving by the hand of his beloved Son. Because of the sacrifice of the Messiah, his blood poured out on the altar of the Cross, we're a free people— free of penalties and punishments chalked up by all our misdeeds. And not just barely free, either. Abundantly free! He thought of everything, provided for everything we could possibly need, letting us in on the plans he took such delight in making. He set it all out before us in Christ, a long-range plan in which everything would be brought together and summed up in him, everything in deepest heaven, and everything on planet earth. It's in Christ that we find out who we are and what we are living for. Long before we first heard of Christ and got our hopes up, he had his eye on us, had designs on us for glorious living, part of the overall purpose he is working out in everything and everyone. (Ephesians 1:3–10 TM)

I know—it's a lot to take in. There is an exuberance here; Paul is waving his arms around and talking so fast we can barely follow the excitement. It has something to do with the plans God has for us. Those plans give God great joy. The heart of those plans is this: To make people whole and holy, by his love. To make *you* whole and holy, by his love. Whole, and holy—this is what you ache for. At least, you ache for the wholeness part. The holy part seems optional. But you will soon see why it is not. Whole and holy—this is your destiny. Once the truth of it seizes you, you'll run around the house whooping at the sheer promise.

Now, we probably all have some idea what wholeness might look like, might even feel like. But what about the holy part? It almost seems a disconnect—summer vacation and clean your room; gelato and Brussels sprouts. What does *this* have to do with *that*? For years I thought of holiness as something austere, spiritually elite, and frankly rather severe. Giving up worldly pleasures, innocent things such as sugar or music or fishing; living an entirely "spiritual" life; praying a lot; being a very good person. Something that only very old saints attain.

In fact, do a little exercise right now—what comes to mind when you read or hear the word *holiness* (that is, as it applies to human beings)? What are your unspoken assumptions about holiness?

This book emerged out of a series of talks I gave to a live audience; at this point I asked them what came to mind when they heard the word *holiness*. These are their words:

Boring
Denial (as in, self-denial)
Discipline
Unattainable
Striving
The goal
Separation (as in from the world or that sort of
    thing)
Hard

I don't think they are an exception. Their response is completely understandable—and heartbreaking. Holiness is not exactly a hot item these days, in great part because we have come to associate all sorts of crushing and unattainable things with it. Yet in order to make human beings what they are meant to be, the love of God seeks to make us whole *and* holy. In fact, the assumption of the New Testament is that you *cannot* become whole without becoming holy; nor can you become holy without becoming whole. The two go hand in hand.

Perhaps there is a rescue waiting for us if we can escape

our misunderstanding of what Christianity is supposed to do to a person, and the role of holiness in that.

CLARIFYING GOD'S INTENTIONS

Let's have a look at an argument that Jesus continues to have with the professional religious of his day. It has to do with the Jewish understanding of the Sabbath. Centuries earlier, God handed down the Law to the Jews (by way of Moses). The fourth commandment stated, "Remember the Sabbath day by keeping it holy" (Exodus 20:8). Correctly observing the Sabbath was for the Jews one of *the* core issues of personal holiness. Getting this right was vital. Getting it wrong could get you nailed to a cross. Now, early in the Gospel of John, Jesus does something that absolutely infuriates the religious leaders of his community:

> Now there is in Jerusalem near the Sheep Gate a pool, which in Aramaic is called Bethesda and which is surrounded by five covered colonnades. Here a great number of disabled people used to lie—the blind, the lame, the paralyzed. One who was there had been an invalid for thirty-eight years. When Jesus saw him lying there and learned that he had been in this condition for a long time, he asked him, "Do you want to get

well?" "Sir," the invalid replied, "I have no one to help me into the pool when the water is stirred. While I am trying to get in, someone else goes down ahead of me." Then Jesus said to him, "Get up! Pick up your mat and walk." At once the man was cured; he picked up his mat and walked. The day on which this took place was a Sabbath, and so the Jews said to the man who had been healed, "It is the Sabbath; the law forbids you to carry your mat." But he replied, "The man who made me well said to me, 'Pick up your mat and walk.'. . . So, because Jesus was doing these things on the Sabbath, the Jews persecuted him. (John 5:2–16)

Jesus heals a man on a Sabbath day, tells him to pick up his mat, and as a result, the religious leadership rages. Two chapters later, Jesus publicly explains his actions:

Jesus answered, "My teaching is not my own. It comes from him who sent me. If anyone chooses to do God's will, he will find out whether my teaching comes from God or whether I speak on my own . . . Has not Moses given you the law? Yet not one of you keeps the law. Why are you trying to kill me?" "You are demon-possessed," the crowd answered. "Who is trying to kill you?" Jesus said to them, "I did one miracle, and you are all astonished. Yet, because Moses gave you circumcision (though actually it did not come from Moses, but from the patriarchs), you circumcise a child on the Sabbath. Now

if a child can be circumcised on the Sabbath so that the law
of Moses may not be broken, why are you angry with me for
healing the whole man on the Sabbath? Stop judging by mere
appearances, and make a right judgment." (John 7:15–24)

Jesus is doing this on purpose. He *waits* until the Sabbath to heal people because he is trying to pierce to the
heart of the issue: "What is God after?" His people—
especially the religious technocrats—have veered pretty
dramatically off course in their religion, beliefs, convictions, passions, and their understanding of what God is
up to. So Jesus provokes the debate by healing on the
Sabbath. He does so as a dramatic illustration of the pur-
poses of God. "This is what I'm up to. I want to heal
the whole man." The healing of the whole man. Do you
see that? The purpose of God is restoring the creation
he made.

That is what Christianity is supposed to do to a person:
restore him as a human being.

God knew what he was doing from the very beginning. He
decided from the outset to shape the lives of those who love
him along the same lines as the life of his Son. The Son stands
first in the line of humanity he restored. We see that original and intended shape of our lives there in him. After God
made that decision of what his children should be like, he fol-

lowed it up by calling people by name. After he called them by name, he set them on a solid base as with himself and then after getting them established, he stayed with them to the end, gloriously completing what he had begun. (Romans 8:29–30)

From the very beginning, God decided to shape our lives along a certain line. The intended shape of our existence is made clear in the person of Jesus. It is a massive undertaking, and notice that it requires *restoration*. "The Son stands first in the line of humanity he restored." Thus, the healing of the whole man. That's the purpose of Christianity.

Now let us jump toward the end of the New Testament (which is the end of the Bible—the whole narrative is drawing to a close). The author of Hebrews is talking about God's processes, his ways with us—both what it feels like at times and, more important, what the *goal* is:

Endure hardship as discipline; God is treating you as sons. For what son is not disciplined by his father? If you are not disciplined (and everyone undergoes discipline), then you are illegitimate children and not true sons. Moreover, we have all had human fathers who disciplined us and we respected them for it. How much more should we submit to the Father of our spirits and live! Our fathers disciplined us for a little while as they thought best; but God disciplines us for our good, that we may share in his holiness. No discipline seems pleasant at the time, but painful. Later on, however, it produces a harvest of righteousness and peace for those who have been trained by it. Therefore, strengthen your feeble arms and weak knees. "Make level paths for your feet," so that the lame may not be disabled, but rather healed. (Hebrews 12:7–13)

Follow this closely now: God is working with us—correcting, guiding, disciplining—so that we might share in his holiness (whatever that is). Therefore, choose your way carefully, so that whatever is broken in you *might be healed*. Severity is not the point; discipline is not the point. The point is the restoration of your creation. Whatever holiness truly is, the *effect* of it is healing. That's what it does to a person.

SIDESHOWS

It seems that much of what Christians believe they are called to these days is a cluster of activities that include regular church attendance, Bible study, prayer, giving, concern for justice, and attending the annual men or women's retreat. Now—what is all that activity *for*? What are those things supposed to do to us, or in us? If it's not restoring the whole man, it may not be in line with what God is doing. Because that's clearly what he's up to. Back to Jesus' argument with the Pharisees. He says,

> "These peoples' heart has become callused. They hardly hear with their ears. They have closed their eyes. Otherwise, they might see with their eyes, hear with their ears, understand with their hearts and turn, and I would heal them."

Do you hear the offer? Do you see what he is so upset about? They have completely missed the point of what God is up to, what he is after in a person's life: to heal him as a human being. This is so essential to your view of the Gospel and your own approach to Christianity. Really—it will shape your convictions about everything else.

It might help to contrast this view with some of the other popular options out there. The Self-Help section in Christian bookstores is rather large now (which is a little ironic, because my books tend to wind up there). This approach has been called—not too kindly but not altogether unfairly—therapeutic Christianity. The goal of this movement seems to be to help you get your life working—help you with your marriage or your anxiety or your loneliness or your weight problems. And it is right and it is wrong. Yes, I believe with all my heart that God helps us with all those things; I believe he wants life for us. But when we focus on fixing problems, what seems to be missing is the transformation of our *character*.

And then you have what we might call righteousness Christianity, quite popular in circles that talk frequently of "sin" and "judgment" and "the loss of morality." A great deal of time and energy here is spent trying to make people behave. And it is right and it is wrong. Of course we're supposed to live godly lives, but where's the joy? Where's the intimacy with God, the "glorious living" that Paul talks about?

Then there's "truth" or "doctrine" Christianity— these are the folks who write books and preach sermons on who's really a heretic and why their own position is the only correct position on salvation, or drinking, or God's sovereignty. The goal in this camp appears to be to ensure correct doctrine in people's lives. And it's right and it's wrong. Of course we should care about the truth. But as the Bible itself warns, you can understand all mysteries and have all knowledge, but if you don't have love, you're obnoxious. This is the noisy gong, the clanging cymbal of 1 Corinthians 13. If you hold the correct doctrinal positions but are irritating to be around, you have sort of missed the point.

Lately, the surge is toward "justice Christianity"— intervening to prevent human trafficking or slavery, car-ing for indigenous cultures or for the planet itself. And it is right and it is wrong. My goodness, yes, of course God cares about justice. But to be frank, it is actually *not* the central theme of the Bible. Christianity isn't simply a religious version of the Peace Corps.

All of these "camps" are Christianity—sort of. Like elevator music is music—sort of. Like veggie burgers are hamburgers—sort of. Think gas fireplaces, wax fruit, frozen burritos. They look like the real thing, but...

It all comes down to this: What is Christianity supposed to do to a person?

> Long before he laid down earth's foundations God had us in mind, had settled on us as the focus of his love to be made whole and holy with his love. (Ephesians 1:4 TM)

God is restoring the creation he made. What you see in Jesus is what he is after in you. This is a really core assumption. Your belief about this will affect the rest of your life.

WHY THE TITLE?

Now, why *The Utter Relief of Holiness*?

It may seem strange at first, because I don't think

most folks look at holiness as an utter relief. Hard, perhaps; boring, if we're honest; necessary, like flossing; a level of spirituality we might attain one day. But a *relief?* Look at it this way: Ask the anorexic young girl how she would feel if she simply no longer struggled with food, diet, exercise—if she simply never even gave it another thought. Ask the man consumed with jealousy how he would feel if he woke one day to discover that all he once felt jealous over was simply gone. Ask the raging person what it would be like to be free of rage or the alcoholic what it would be like to be completely free from addiction. Take the things you struggle with and ask yourself, "What would life be like if I never struggled with this again?"

It would be an utter relief. An absolute, utter relief.

Exactly. Now, in order to get there, you need both wholeness and holiness. You can't find genuine wholeness without genuine goodness; that's why the therapeutic Christianity camp seems to be missing something essential. I know a lot of folks who are chasing wholeness, but they don't seem to be concerned about their holiness. The same holds true for the folks who think wholeness is a distraction, maybe humanistic; they feel the focus needs to be on pursuing righteousness or moral living. And I can promise you, there isn't a snowball's chance in hell of you becoming the person God made you to be without the healing of your humanity. You can't get to holiness without wholeness. The two go together.

I think if we could recover a vision of what holiness actually is, we would be absolutely captured by it. I think we would see it as not only completely desirable, but attainable as well. King David was a man who knew his character flaws, felt the anguish of regret, spent many a tormented night wrestling with his failings. And yet, in Psalm 119, David wrote this:

> "I run in the path of your commands, because you have set my heart free."

Have you ever put those two things together—freedom of heart and the passionate pursuit of God's commands? The two go hand in hand. Genuine holiness restores human beings; restored human beings possess genuine holiness.

CHAPTER TWO

The Compelling Goodness of Jesus

Then Jesus entered and walked through Jericho. There was a man there, his name Zacchaeus, the head tax man and quite rich. He wanted desperately to see Jesus, but the crowd was in his way—he was a short man and couldn't see over the crowd. So he ran on ahead and climbed up in a sycamore tree so he could see Jesus when he came by. When Jesus got to the tree, he looked up and said, "Zacchaeus, hurry down. Today is my day to be a guest in your home." Zacchaeus scrambled out of the tree, hardly believing his good luck, delighted to take Jesus home with him. Everyone who saw the incident was indignant and grumped, "What business does he have getting cozy with this crook?" Zacchaeus just stood there, a little stunned. He stammered apologetically, "Master, I give away half my income to the poor—and if I'm caught cheating, I pay four times the damages." Jesus said, "Today is salvation day in this home! Here he is: Zacchaeus, son of Abraham!

For the Son of Man came to find and restore the lost." (Luke 19:1–10 TM)

I love this story. It is so unexpected, and funny, and so . . . whimsical. Here's this short guy—picture Danny DeVito—who frankly is a bit of a traitor and a swindler. Though a Jew, he has sided with the Roman occupation forces, extracting Caesar's taxes from his countrymen and skimming a little off the top for himself. Jesus is passing through town; the little man tries to get to the front of the row, but the crowd—they hate tax collectors—shove him back. So he runs ahead of the caravan and . . . climbs a tree?! In his full-length Armani robe? Why does Zacchaeus find Jesus so compelling? He "wanted desperately to see Jesus." Fascinating. Apparently, he's either heard stories about this man—from fellow bill collector Matthew maybe?—or he's seen him from a distance before, and now he simply must get a closer look.

The next moment is as rich as the Gospels get: Jesus pauses under the tree and looks up. Oh, to have seen the expression on Jesus' face—the twinkle in his eye, the slight grin behind the serious command. He knows what this is going to do to the little pirate's world.

"C'mon down, Zacchaeus." (How did he know
  his name?!)
"I'm having lunch at your house." (He invites
  himself over?!)

Oh, the beautifully disruptive ways of Jesus. Disruptive
both for the crowd ("What business does he have getting
cozy with this crook?") and for the little extortionist, too.
Zacchaeus' reaction is so utterly extravagant we never see
it coming: "I give away half my savings to the poor."
What? Have you been around money people much? Let
me remind you that it is a *fool* and his money that are
soon parted; the rich and clever are never separated from
theirs. When they do give way to a philanthropic urge,
they are always certain to get a tax deduction. On the
spot, Zacchaeus cuts his lifestyle, his portfolio, and his
retirement *in half*? Then he goes on to promise a total
change of life?

Wow.

There was, obviously, something about Jesus, some
wonderful quality that compelled people to *want* to be
good.

And this is where we must begin our search for holiness. Not with pressure, nor with shame or command.
The only lasting change is the kind that seized Zacchaeus, and this comes by way of Jesus. The best thing we

can do is push our way to the front of the crowd—or scale a tree—and have a closer look ourselves.[1]

The Goodness of Jesus

If you were to write a history of men—the true history, not the popular one clouded by kings and conquests—you would want to write the story of the *internal* world of men. And a fascinating story it would be, too. What makes men tick? Why do they do the things they do? What is it that truly sets great men apart? Thus far the book has not been written, but if you were to undertake the quest, I think the pressing question would be this one: What can you trust him with? That is the test of any man's character. Over the ages, the answer appears to be: not much. Certainly not the sirens of power, fame, or pleasure. Men have sold their countries for a night of sex and their daughters for an ounce of heroin. And so I find it intriguing that the Gospels introduce Jesus the man with two events—one public, the other very private.

First, we have his baptism:

---

1. Now, for a far fuller encounter with Jesus, you'll want to read *Beautiful Outlaw*. There I have an entire book to unveil what we have only a chapter for here. This is the glance from the sycamore; that is having Jesus over to spend a few weeks at your house.

Then Jesus came from Galilee to the Jordan to be baptized by John. But John tried to deter him, saying, "I need to be baptized by you, and do you come to me?" Jesus replied, "Let it be so now; it is proper for us to do this to fulfill all righteousness." Then John consented. (Matthew 3:13–15)

Now, to grasp the significance of the moment, you must keep in mind that John the Baptist has taken the lead. It is his revival that has the whole countryside buzzing. Jesus simply shows up one day, gets in line like a carpenter on his lunch break, and lets John dunk him. Then he disappears into the crowd. No fanfare, no changing of the guard. Compare it to a presidential primary, or the Academy Awards—this is not exactly how world leaders typically act. Jesus' *humility* is almost breathtaking.

What follows is even more extraordinary:

Now Jesus, full of the Holy Spirit, left the Jordan and was led by the Spirit into the wild. For forty wilderness days and nights he was tested by the Devil. He ate nothing during those days, and when the time was up he was hungry. The Devil, playing on his hunger, gave the first test: "Since you're God's Son, command this stone to turn into a loaf of bread." Jesus answered by quoting Deuteronomy: "It takes more than bread to really live." For the second test he led him up and spread out all the kingdoms of the earth on display at once. Then the Devil said, "They're yours in all their splendor to serve your pleasure. I'm in charge of them all and can turn them over to whomever I wish. Worship me and they're yours, the whole works." Jesus refused, again backing his refusal with Deuteronomy: "Worship the Lord your God and only the Lord your God. Serve him with absolute single-heartedness." For the third test the Devil took him to Jerusalem and put him on top of the Temple. He said, "If you are God's Son, jump. It's written, isn't it, that 'he has placed you in the care of angels to protect you; they will catch you; you won't so much as stub your toe on a stone'?" "Yes," said Jesus, "and it's also written, 'Don't you dare tempt the Lord your God.'" That completed the testing. The Devil retreated temporarily, lying in wait for another opportunity. Jesus returned to Galilee powerful in the Spirit. (Luke 4:1–14 TM)

First off, this is a backroom offer; this all took place far from Jerusalem, far from any observer. No one needs to know; no one will ever know. The first seduction almost seems innocuous: make yourself something to eat. Jesus is famished and bread isn't exactly adultery. Oh, the subtleties of the evil one. The issue? When you are famished for anything—love, attention, relief from pain, security—will you continue to trust God or will you take matters into your own hands? "There are always options," whispers the Deceiver. "No," replies Jesus. Then the evil one tries overwhelming seduction; surely every man has his price. "No deal," says Jesus. The third attempt seems truly bizarre, until you see that the enemy has got Jesus' number—he sees that this man is committed to total trust in his Father. "Prove it," the devil says, "and jump." Jesus is immovable.

Why do the scriptures begin the story of Jesus of Nazareth here?

Look at it this way—Jesus is asking you to trust him at a very profound level, trust him with everything that is dear to you, trust him with your own soul. So the witness begins with a revelation of his *character*—genuine humility and unstained integrity. Is this what you expect from your leaders; is this what you assume around election time? It is remarkable. This man's heart is so good; this is someone we can trust.

In fact, if you begin with the question of genuine goodness, you quickly discover running through every story in the Gospels the shimmering substance of Jesus' character.

WOMEN

Here's something I think most people have never seen before. This moment takes place on Easter morning. Jesus of Nazareth has been systematically tortured and then hung by his hands and feet from timbers. He died, and his body quickly laid in a borrowed tomb. But early Sunday morning, the event that changed the history of mankind took place without even a single witness: Jesus was raised from the dead. If it were you, whom would you want to show yourself to first? Part of me says, "Those religious bullies, the oppressors of my people, the ones who sent me to my death—that'll shock the hell out of them" (which is, of course, exactly what needs shocking out of them). His closest friends come to mind; they are devastated. Wouldn't you rush to share the good news? Then I think, "No—it would be best to show myself to the crowds still in the city; this is the moment of moments to get the conversions rolling, to start the revolution that will be called Christianity. And of course, there is my mother; she is heartbroken." Whom does Jesus choose?

He appears first, and privately, to Mary Magdalene:

No one yet knew from the Scripture that he had to rise from the dead. The disciples then went back home. But Mary stood outside the tomb weeping. As she wept, she knelt to look into the tomb and saw two angels sitting there, dressed in white, one at the head, the other at the foot of where Jesus' body had been laid. They said to her, "Woman, why do you weep?" "They took my Master," she said, "and I don't know where they put him." After she said this, she turned away and saw Jesus standing there. But she didn't recognize him. Jesus spoke to her, "Woman, why do you weep? Who are you looking for?" She, thinking that he was the gardener, said, "Mister, if you took him, tell me where you put him so I can care for him." Jesus said, "Mary." (John 20:9–16)

So much, so very much spoken in just one word, her name: Mary. This is an incredibly beautiful scene. There must have been something particularly sweet and deep in their relationship for Jesus to have chosen her as the first person he wanted to speak to after coming back to life. And it is this—Jesus' ability to have intimate relationships with single women—that is really striking. His capacity to engage the opposite sex with absolute integrity and utter fearlessness is incredible. We've had presidents who couldn't be trusted on this front for two minutes; it has been the snare of many a pastor as well. As a result, there is a good deal of fear and awkwardness between men and women who are not married to each other. Especially in the Church. But Jesus is showing that it needn't even be an issue. Wow!

His retinue includes a number of women traveling with him (very, very unusual in that day). Prostitutes throw themselves at his feet. And how about the story of his encounter with the single woman whom he meets by a well. I love this story. She is, shall we say, not exactly strict with her sexual boundaries. Jesus engages her in conversation (which is itself a shocking move; no rabbi would ever have done this). She's suspicious, defensive, and then... well, she seems to think that Jesus has something else in mind. He senses the shift and says to her, "Go call your husband and come back." She replies that she has no husband—which is technically true, though she has had five and is currently living with a man. Why does she hide this information? This is a scandalous scene. And I love Jesus' integrity: he is neither seduced nor frightened. He continues to pursue her heart and eventually wins her to the Kingdom of God.

We are witnessing something here that goes beyond good behavior. This genuine holiness is flowing from deep within; Jesus is saturated with it.

POWER

Then there is the question of how a man handles power—fame, popularity, influence. As I mentioned, the

Gospels begin not with Jesus but with his cousin John the Baptist; it is John who gets the revival rolling. Then Jesus' ministry begins to take hold and quickly overtakes and surpasses John's (which is of course the very thing John *wanted* to happen). It is an awkward moment, however. Watch how Jesus handles it in an overlooked passage from the fourth Gospel:

> Jesus realized that the Pharisees were keeping count of the baptisms that he and John performed (although his disciples, not Jesus, did the actual baptizing). They had posted the score that Jesus was ahead, turning him and John into rivals in the eyes of the people. So Jesus left the Judean countryside and went back to Galilee. (John 4:1–3)

He just up and leaves? Right when his movement is gaining momentum? This is classic Jesus. As soon as popularity surges in one town, Jesus leaves and heads someplace that is three or four days' journey away. On Palm Sunday he enters Jerusalem to cheering throngs; that night, he ducks out of town and stays in a humble village with a few close friends. His humility is just remarkable; there is deference here, modesty that is so holy.

> Later they sent some of the Pharisees and Herodians to Jesus to catch him in his words. They came to him and said,

"Teacher, we know you are a man of integrity. You aren't swayed by men, because you pay no attention to who they are; but you teach the way of God in accordance with the truth. Is it right to pay taxes to Caesar or not? Should we pay or shouldn't we?" But Jesus knew their hypocrisy. "Why are you trying to trap me?" he asked. "Bring me a denarius and let me look at it." They brought the coin, and he asked them, "Whose portrait is this? And whose inscription?" "Caesar's," they replied. Then Jesus said to them, "Give to Caesar what is Caesar's and to God what is God's." And they were amazed at him. (Mark 12:13–17)

We see here that it is not false humility. Jesus doesn't cuddle up to flattery. "Teacher, we know you are a man of integrity blah blah blah." Most of us soften in the face of flattery, but not Jesus. Again, this is *so* rare among the rich and famous. Most leaders surround themselves with those who flatter them.

When Jesus had called the Twelve together, he gave them power and authority to drive out all demons and to cure diseases, and he sent them out to preach the kingdom of God and to heal the sick . . . So they set out and went from village to village, preaching the gospel and healing people everywhere. (Luke 9:1, 6)

Now this is just extraordinary—Jesus has absolutely no need to be the center of the action. He sends his friends out to do the very things he does; he gives them a major role in his campaign. "You go do it. Do everything you see me doing." This is humble and this is extraordinarily generous; Jesus is absolutely openhanded with his kingdom. There is no need for the whole thing to be always about him. He is absolutely delighted to share his kingdom with us. He later says, "Don't be afraid little ones; your father is delighted to give you the kingdom."

Most men get power and then crave more; as their stars rise they can't bear to have others in the spotlight; they typically abuse the power they have; and in the end, it winds up crushing them and everyone around them. You recall the expression "Power corrupts, and absolute power corrupts absolutely." It was a lesson learned through the long soiled history of men and power. But then we have Jesus, who walks right through the snares as if they weren't even there, handling immense power with casual grace.

PEOPLE

But far and above the most revealing aspect of anyone's character is how he handles people. Friends, I hope you understand this—the way a person handles others is the acid test of his true nature. How is Jesus with people? What's he like to be around?

> One day children were brought to Jesus in the hope that he would lay hands on them and pray over them. The disciples shooed them off. But Jesus intervened: "Let the children alone, don't prevent them from coming to me. God's kingdom is made up of people like these." After laying hands on them, he left. (Matthew 19:13–14 TM)

A simple story, very Sunday school. But we've made a precious moment out of it, and thus missed both the reality and the beauty. Our church held a meeting last week, and apparently child care wasn't available, because the little ones were dashing up and down the halls and, once in a while, in and through the middle of the gathering. Most people tried to put a good face on it, but after several interruptions, you could feel the irritation. The mood shifted from *How cute* at the first interruption, to *That's enough of that* at the third, to, *Little nuisance—where are your parents?* by romp number five. I indulged in the irritation myself. This is at the core of human nature, this thing in us that growls, *Do not mess with my program. Do not get in my way.* If you aren't aware how deep this runs in you, how do you feel when people cut in the line at the market or the movies, cut you off on the highway, make it difficult for you to get your job done, or make it impossible for you to get some sleep? What angers us is almost always some version of *You are making my life even harder than it already is. Get out of the way.*

Not Jesus. He welcomes intrusion.

In Luke's version of the story, the disciples succeed in shooing off both parents and tykes, but Jesus "called them back." Later Jesus passes two blind men on the road; they create a ruckus in order to get his attention. His handlers try to shut them up. But Jesus stops what he's doing and gives them his undivided attention. Do you recall the wedding at Cana, where he turned water into wine? By Jesus' own words, it is clear he had not intended to reveal himself at the time, in that way. But his mom asked, and the groom was in a tight spot, and the party would have died far too soon, so he does it anyway. To the tune of 180 gallons of wine! He's such an immensely gracious person. I love him for that. I yearn to be like that.

> Meanwhile in Capernaum, there was a certain official from the king's court whose son was sick. When he heard that Jesus had come from Judea to Galilee, he went and asked that he come down and heal his son, who was on the brink of death. Jesus put him off: "Unless you people are dazzled by a miracle, you refuse to believe." But the court official wouldn't be put

off. "Come down! It's life or death for my son." Jesus simply replied, "Go home. Your son lives." On his way back, his servants intercepted him and announced, "Your son lives!" He asked them what time he began to get better. They said, "The fever broke yesterday afternoon at one o'clock." The father knew that that was the very moment Jesus had said, "Your son lives." (John 4:46–53 TM)

What we see here is his kindness in spite of the fact that people don't get him or the purpose of his coming. They aren't putting their lives in his hands; they're hoping for some help and that's it. Jesus is clearly grieved by the fact that these people continue to ask for miracles but have no intention of becoming his followers. Yet he heals for them anyway. His immense goodness is what captures me. He is, after all, the one who said, "Love your enemies and pray for those who persecute you" (Matthew 5:44). He's probably also the only one who's ever done it consistently.

On and on the stories go. Denied and abandoned by Peter, Jesus doesn't hold it against him. Tortured mercilessly, he says, "Forgive them, Father, they don't know what they do." Look, I think I can eventually get around to forgiving people—so long as they ask me to, apologize, and seem genuinely sorry. But Jesus forgives his executors before there's even a hint of remorse.

Wouldn't you love to live like that?

What you are seeing in any one of these stories is holiness. I think if anyone of us could have known Jesus personally, in that day, we would have loved his company—his ability to navigate difficult situations, to deal with people who didn't know how to deal with him, engage the opposite sex, take on the religious leaders with the right spirit and attitude. It's just astounding. One more thing—Jesus isn't gutting it through life. There is no sense of him gritting his teeth, biting his tongue, none of that internal anguish most of us require to pull this off for a day or two. He is walking through it all with such grace and strength. He is living life as it was meant to be lived.

That's the utter relief of holiness.

And, oh, how utterly attractive it is.

GENUINE GOODNESS IS *CAPTIVATING*

You can tell a lot about a person by his effect on others. What is he like to be around? What is the aftertaste he leaves in your mouth? Is this someone you'd want to take a long car ride with? We saw Zacchaeus' reaction. Here are two more, from people quite different from each other and from Zacchaeus:

One of the Pharisees asked him over for a meal. He went to
the Pharisee's house and sat down at the dinner table. Just then
a woman of the village, the town harlot, having learned that
Jesus was a guest in the home of the Pharisee, came with a
bottle of very expensive perfume and stood at his feet, weeping, raining tears on his feet. Letting down her hair, she dried
his feet, kissed them, and anointed them with the perfume.
(Luke 7:36–38 TM)

No comment of mine could add to the beauty of this
moment. Nor to this one:

Two others, both criminals, were taken along with him for
execution. When they got to the place called Skull Hill, they
crucified him, along with the criminals, one on his right, the
other on his left. Jesus prayed, "Father, forgive them; they
don't know what they're doing." The people stood there star-
ing at Jesus, and the ringleaders made faces, taunting, "He
saved others. Let's see him save himself! The Messiah of
God—ha! The Chosen—ha!" The soldiers also came up and
poked fun at him, making a game of it. They toasted him
with sour wine: "So you're King of the Jews! Save yourself!"
Printed over him was a sign: this is the king of the jews. One
of the criminals hanging alongside cursed him: "Some Messiah you are! Save yourself! Save us!" But the other one made
him shut up: "Have you no fear of God? You're getting the

same as him. We deserve this, but not him—he did nothing to deserve this." Then he said, "Jesus, remember me when you enter your kingdom." He said, "Don't worry, I will. Today you will join me in paradise." (Luke 23:32–43 TM)

What is stunning to see in these brief accounts is that people who *knew* themselves to be anything but holy found the holiness of Jesus winsome, open-armed, and utterly compelling.

Is this how you have understood holiness?

It changes everything when you do.

CHAPTER THREE

Set Free to Live

I received this note from a friend last week:

I think it began with traffic, my response to traffic. The way people drive, how stupid they can be. I noticed I was having a pretty strong reaction to it. *You are such a *@#%! idiot.* It felt good, my reaction felt good; it felt justified. I could let some steam off. But then I began to notice a similar pattern at work. Somebody would send around one of those lame corporate emails, and it would be filled with such stupid decisions and backward ideas it would just fry me; I wanted to fire back. Sometimes I did. More often than not I'd just write the email and then delete it. Something was really pissed off inside of me. Then I saw it in my friendships, especially when people would let me down. I wanted to point out what they were doing; it felt the same as on the freeway. I wanted to fry them. I began to see that resentment was a pretty deep part of my experience in the world. When I'd hear of bad news that had struck someone, I wouldn't feel compassion; I'd feel like, *Maybe now you'll get your act together.* It was a horrible feeling. My God—am I such a bad person? I felt torn inside, like part of me was just hurt and another part of me was resentful. Why am I such an angry person? Why am I so resentful? It's tearing me apart.

This is a horrible place to find yourself in. Substitute lust or envy, fear or resignation, compulsion of any kind, and you'll find yourself saying words like these, I have no doubt.

My friend isn't crying out for vengeance, or for dominance. He's crying out for *goodness.* Our souls will never be right without it. That is why goodness is the healing of our humanity. It really is.

Another friend I'll call Susan used to be quite an accomplished liar. All through her youth, but certainly in her teenage years, she was a compulsive liar. And the terrible thing is, she was very, very good at it. She has something close to a photographic memory—essential for a liar if she is never to be found out. She would lie to her parents about where she'd been; lie to her teachers as to why she'd missed class; lie to boys in order to gain their favor; lie to impress her friends. As I write these words, I am on the one hand deeply embarrassed for my friend, and on the other hand, it feels like I am describing someone else. It has been quite a few years now since Jesus Christ got hold of Susan's life, and the thought of telling even the most "innocent white lie" is now repulsive to her. No, that's not quite it; I think I could honestly say she simply isn't even capable of it. She hates falsehood in any form. I love that about her. The professional liar can't help but tell the truth these days.

My friend "Benny" was a drug dealer in his twenties. Hash, marijuana, cocaine, acid, amphetamines, barbiturates—you name it, he brokered it all. And made a killing. The guy was rolling in cash. Utterly bereft of conscience, indifferent to the devastation he was causing, Benny became rich by encouraging chemical dependencies in hundreds of people—addictions that destroyed many of their lives. "Most of my friends are dead," Benny confessed one day. "The others are in mental wards. They overdosed." Thirty years ago Jesus Christ took hold of Benny's life in a fairly dramatic way, and now the pusher can't bear to take an aspirin. He's a kind, compassionate man who would do anything to see his friends restored. The money, the drugs, and the lifestyle that went with it all are simply gone. Vanished. "I don't even remember that person anymore," Benny says, grateful and humbled.

"David" was known as an upstanding member of his church and a generous philanthropist. His business acumen and Christian testimony won him positions on many boards of directors—a hospital, several ministries, the local Christian school his children attended. In his secret life, he visited prostitutes several times a week; he sat in seedy pornographic cinemas in the middle of the afternoon; he was thoroughly addicted to alcohol; he practiced a number of unethical business deals. The crash came hard. A colleague exposed David, and it pretty much destroyed his family. His wife was a daughter of missionaries, a saint if ever there was one. It broke her heart, and she spiraled into a three-year depression. One of his daughters became a prostitute herself. His son had a police record. And now? David is a humble, gentle man with no sexual addictions. He has been sober for three years; the thought of a drink makes him nauseated.

> God knew what he was doing from the very beginning. He decided from the outset to shape the lives of those who love him along the same line as the line of his son. The Son stands first in the line of humanity he restored. (Romans 8:29 TM)

Before we go any further in our search, I need to make the offer of Christianity clear: There is a way to be good again. The hope of Christianity is that we get to live life like Jesus. That beautiful goodness can be ours. He can heal what has gone wrong deep inside each of us. The way he does this is to give us *his* goodness; impart it to us, almost like a blood transfusion or mouth-to-mouth resuscitation. We get to live *his* life—that is, live each day by the power of his life within us. That's the hope: you get to live that life. "But there is a reality of being in which all things are easy and plain," wrote George MacDonald, "oneness, that is, with the Lord of life." He makes us whole by making us holy. He makes us holy by making us whole.

Think of how you feel when you commit some offense—yell at your kids, lie to someone or hide the full truth, harbor resentment or bitterness toward a friend, indulge sexual or romantic fantasies over someone at work or their spouse; maybe you've been acting on those fantasies for three years now and it is tearing you apart. Whatever your regrets may be, think of how you feel when you commit these acts repeatedly, when you vow never to do it again and find yourself doing it moments later. And think of what an utter relief it would be to be free from the whole entangled nightmare. I mean to be so free that you're not even disciplining yourself not to do these things anymore; you just don't do them. You simply don't struggle with whatever it is that haunts you; it's not an issue.

That's the utter relief of holiness. That's what happens when the life of Jesus invades your life.

CHAPTER FOUR

JESUS ON HOLINESS

You are the salt of the earth. But if the salt loses its saltiness, how can it be made salty again? It is no longer good for anything, except to be thrown out and trampled by men. You are the light of the world. A city on a hill cannot be hidden. Neither do people light a lamp and put it under a bowl. Instead they put it on its stand, and it gives light to everyone in the house. In the same way, let your light shine before men, that they may see your good deeds and praise your Father in heaven. Do not think that I have come to abolish the Law or the Prophets; I have not come to abolish them but to fulfill them. I tell you the truth, until heaven and earth disappear, not the smallest letter, not the least stroke of a pen, will by any means disappear from the Law until everything is accomplished. Anyone who breaks one of the least of these commandments and teaches others to do the same will be called least in the kingdom of heaven, but whoever practices

and teaches these commands will be called great in the kingdom of heaven. For I tell you that unless your righteousness
surpasses that of the Pharisees and the teachers of the law,
you will certainly not enter the kingdom of heaven. (Matthew
5:13–20)

Well, now—that's pretty straightforward. And unnerv-
ing. The Master of all Goodness is making a few things
absolutely clear in his famous lecture from the mountainside. First off, that goodness *matters*. Immensely. Far more
than you think it does. In fact, he goes on to connect
your personal holiness with your entrance into the kingdom of heaven. Uh-oh.

Now, I know my fellow evangelicals will rush to
protest that it is the cross of Jesus Christ alone that opens
the way to heaven for any person. No amount of personal righteousness could ever suffice. I believe this. It is
grace alone—the unmerited and undeserved forgiveness
of God—that opens the way for any of us to know God,
let alone come into his kingdom. "For it is by grace you
have been saved, through faith—and this not from yourselves, it is the gift of God—not by works, so that no one
can boast" (Ephesians 2:8–9). Thank God for that.

However, you also find in Jesus and throughout the
scriptures a pretty serious call to a holy life.

Make every effort to live in peace with all men and to be holy;
without holiness no one will see the Lord. (Hebrews 12:14)

For God did not call us to be impure, but to live a holy life.
(1 Thessalonians 4:7)

As obedient children, do not conform to the evil desires you
had when you lived in ignorance. But just as he who called
you is holy, so be holy in all you do; for it is written: "Be holy,
because I am holy." (1 Peter 1:14–16)

In fact, one of the most stunning things about Jesus
is how such a gracious, kind, patient, and forgiving man
holds—without so much as wavering—such a high standard of holiness. On the one hand, we have the beautiful
story of a woman caught in the act of adultery—and
how horrifying and humiliating would that be? The mob
drags her before Jesus, ready to stone her (they actually
did this sort of thing, and not that long ago; it still happens in some Muslim countries today). Jesus disarms the
violence in a most cunning way:

The religion scholars and Pharisees led in a woman who had
been caught in an act of adultery. They stood her in plain sight
of everyone and said, "Teacher, this woman was caught red-
handed in the act of adultery. Moses, in the Law, gives orders

to stone such persons. What do you say?" They were trying to trap him into saying something incriminating so they could bring charges against him. They kept at him, badgering him. He straightened up and said, "The sinless one among you, go first: Throw the stone." Bending down again, he wrote some more in the dirt. Hearing that, they walked away, one after another, beginning with the oldest. The woman was left alone. Jesus stood up and spoke to her. "Woman, where are they? Does no one condemn you?" "No one, Master." "Neither do I," said Jesus. (John 8:3–10 TM)

It is brilliant, and poignant. The town square is now deserted; only the woman and Jesus remain. She is probably wrapped in nothing but a bed sheet and her shame. He rescues her from a terrible death, and then forgives her. It feels as if the scene could not be more powerfully reported. What more could be said? But wait, Jesus has one last word for her:

"Go on your way. From now on, don't sin."

Yes, grace reigns in the Kingdom of God. But right there alongside it is an unflinching call to holiness. Go and sin no more. You see something equally startling (and much less anticipated) at the end of a story I recounted earlier, where Jesus healed the man on the Sabbath and told him to take up his mat. The rest of the story reads like this:

> The man was healed on the spot. He picked up his bedroll and walked off. The Jews stopped the healed man and said, "It's the Sabbath. You can't carry your bedroll around. It's against the rules." But he told them, "The man who made me well told me to. He said, 'Take your bedroll and start walking.'" They asked, "Who gave you the order to take it up and start walking?" But the healed man didn't know, for Jesus had slipped away into the crowd. A little later Jesus found him in the Temple and said, "You look wonderful! You're well! Don't return to a sinning life or something worse might happen." (John 5:9–14 TM)

It is nearly comical in its extreme juxtaposition. "I'm so glad you are well! Now stop sinning, or something really bad is going to come down on you!"

Imagine the family gathered by grandfather's bedside. The old man is dying. The neighborhood priest steps quietly into the room. But instead of administering last rites, he prays for grandpa—and lo and behold! The cantankerous old coot is healed! The family is stunned; then follows the rejoicing and glad tears. The priest simply smiles and slips out, leaving them to their incredulity and joy. Later that evening he comes back to the bedside; Grandfather is up and having a robust meal. He looks splendid. The priest smiles. "I'm so happy God did this for you, Roger. What a wonderful thing—you have your life back!" And then: "Now, listen, you old grouch—the heavy drinking has got to stop; so does your abusive language toward your wife; and the way you use guilt to manipulate your children. You'd better clean up your act or one morning you'll step out of bed and drop straight into hell. Have a nice evening."

That's pretty much the effect of Jesus' warnings at the end of such marvelous stories. Actually, he does this sort of thing frequently. And yet I can't think of anyone else remotely like this man.

Most Christians desire very deeply to be known as gracious, kind, patient, and forgiving. We feel we "owe" it to Jesus to be seen on our best behavior. This is even truer for those of us in "the ministry," whose lives are publicly attached to Jesus. Now, some of the motivation behind this is beautiful (we'll look at the rest in a moment). We know how horribly religion has distorted the world's view of God, and we want very much to gain a hearing for Jesus, so we go to great lengths to reassure the wary that those aligned with Jesus are really great people. In fact, nowadays most Christian leaders bend over backward to come across as very cool and hip and in no way whatsoever judgmental or condemning. It's the new PR campaign for Jesus.

The problem is, in our efforts to be good poster children for Christianity, we have sort of hidden or left off this other side of Jesus' personality. The man is dead serious about holiness.

> "Woe to you, teachers of the law and Pharisees, you hypocrites! You clean the outside of the cup and dish, but inside they are full of greed and self-indulgence. Blind Pharisee! First clean the inside of the cup and dish, and then the outside also will be clean. Woe to you, teachers of the law and Pharisees, you hypocrites! You are like whitewashed tombs, which look beautiful on the outside but on the inside are full of dead men's bones and everything unclean. In the same way, on the outside you appear to people as righteous but on the inside you are full of hypocrisy and wickedness." (Matthew 23:25–28)

I would love to have heard his tone of voice, seen the expression on his face. I think we can be fairly confident that when Jesus thundered, "Woe to you," everyone just about peed their pants. And what is the issue here? Shallow holiness. Faking it. Ignoring the deeper issues of the soul. As far as Jesus is concerned, holiness is a matter of the heart. "Clean the inside of the cup and dish, and the outside will be clean as well." The model of personal transformation that Christianity offers is internal to external. It's a transformation of the heart, the mind, the

will, the soul—which then begins to express itself exter-
nally in our actions. This is absolutely critical in order to
understand Jesus and his genuine goodness.

Which, I feel I need to remind you, was utterly captivating. Let's not lose hold of that as we press a bit deeper.

A Matter of the Heart

"You have heard that it was said to the people long ago,
'Do not murder, and anyone who murders will be subject to
judgment.' But I tell you that anyone who is angry with his
brother will be subject to judgment...

"You have heard that it was said, 'Do not commit adultery.'
But I tell you that anyone who looks at a woman lustfully has
already committed adultery with her in his heart...

"Be careful not to do your 'acts of righteousness' before
men, to be seen by them. If you do, you will have no reward
from your Father in heaven. So when you give to the needy,
do not announce it with trumpets, as the hypocrites do in
the synagogues and on the streets, to be honored by men. I
tell you the truth, they have received their reward in full. But
when you give to the needy, do not let your left hand know
what your right hand is doing, so that your giving may be in
secret. Then your Father, who sees what is done in secret, will
reward you...

"And when you pray, do not be like the hypocrites, for they love to pray standing in the synagogues and on the street corners to be seen by men. I tell you the truth, they have received their reward in full. But when you pray, go into your room, close the door and pray to your Father, who is unseen. Then your Father, who sees what is done in secret, will reward you." (Matthew 5:21–22, 27–28; 6:1–6)

The Sermon on the Mount is a revolution in holiness. Jesus takes all the external issues and makes them first and foremost *internal*. He begins with a few examples of the most egregious sins: murder and adultery. This is a crowd that congratulates itself on staying far from such obvious crimes. But then Jesus says, "Oh—don't think you've kept the command simply because you haven't pulled the trigger. If you hate someone, you've murdered them in your heart. And as for sexual integrity—just because you haven't actually 'done it' doesn't mean you're clean—have you *wanted* to, in your heart? Have you desired someone who wasn't your spouse?"

Gulp.

This way of looking at goodness is mighty exposing. As it should be. Holiness, he is driving at, is a matter of the heart.

To make it practical, Jesus gives us the category of motive. Whatever else the sermon is about, whatever goodness is truly about, motive will get you there. Motives are essential, and taking this path will open up fields of goodness for you.

I've noticed at the retreats we do, I am very careful to be kind and attentive to people. Though I am often tired, and spent, I try my best to treat every question with respect. But what is my motive? It could be love. But it also could be that I want to be *seen as* kind and attentive. Same action, different motives. You can't really tell from the outside; what matters is what's going on *inside*. I spent a lot of time working on this book. Why? Well, it could be because I want to try to present these things to you as helpfully as I can; it could also be that I want to impress you, or be thought well of, or simply avoid embarrassment. One motive is loving; the others are self-serving.

This is why Jesus pushed into the issue of our motives; genuine goodness isn't skin deep. Motive is a *very* essential category.

Mary is a woman who loves to help people. She's always the one to stay and clean up after a party; she'll make copies for the meeting; she's always happy to take your call. In fact, she loves to be asked. But over time I noticed something: Mary will serve long and hard, as long as Mary is in the center of the action. If someone else is telling a story, she doesn't really pay attention; if someone else is doing the serving, she sort of wanders around on the sidelines with a bit of a hurt expression. The truth is, Mary is good so long as she's needed, even needed to carry heavy burdens. But it's still about Mary; when it's about someone else, she isn't present at all. What looks like service is really her way of getting herself needed and noticed. That's not goodness at all.

Think about how you operate in social settings—why don't you want to be seen talking to Fred? Is it because Fred is unpopular and laughed at by the "in" crowd. Why do you move directly toward Joan and Harold? Is it because they are part of the "in" crowd? You flatter your boss—is it because you really like what he's said, or because next week is your performance review? Why do you use such highly technical language in a business meeting? Is it truly helpful to your listeners—or does it give you the aura of being the "expert," allow you to throw some terms around to impress others? Maybe you don't speak up in a meeting at all—why is that? Is it humility, or is it simply fear?

The phone rings; you check caller ID and don't answer it. You satisfy yourself by thinking, "Well, we are in the middle of dinner." But the real motive is you are avoiding that person. You have something to say to a friend or a co-worker; you choose e-mail to say it. Why? Because it will help that person better understand the issue? Or because you haven't the courage to tell him to his face? Isn't it easier to take shots from a distance? You laugh at your neighbor's jokes during the annual Christmas party; yet you hate your neighbor. So what's with the pretending?

You are faithful in attending church. Why? Is it because you are truly worshiping God there? Or could it be because you know people will "talk" if you don't? Speaking of church, why the joke in the sermon? Is it really part of the message God gave you—or does it serve to win the crowd, make the congregation like you? We get angry when our children misbehave in public. Why? Isn't it really because it is embarrassing, because the crowd is now looking at us and forming opinions about us as parents? I want my sons to be seen as spiritual. Why? Could the fact that I'm a Christian author and leader of a ministry be playing a role in that—or is it truly a longing for them to walk with God?

Friends, until we begin to get honest about our motives, we are kidding ourselves about holiness. We are pretending.

1Motives

Most of my readers probably remember the commercials comparing the Mac to the PC. "Hello. I'm a Mac." "And

I'm a PC." They were funny; they were clever; they were absolutely brilliant. The Mac was hip, laid-back, dressed for the times, tolerant, "authentic," the ultimate postmodern. The PC was awkward, dressed for the office climate of the 1980s, goofy, overweight, fumbling, and clearly *not* authentic. C'mon now, admit it—you wanted to be the Mac. Even if you didn't own a Mac computer or ever cared to own a Mac, in that commercial, you wanted to be the Mac. Who wants to be the schlub?

Surely you are aware what a powerful motive "wanting to be liked" is. It shapes what you wear every day. The way you talk. The way you present yourself to the world. What you say. What you won't say. How you want to be seen. Your opinions. In the powerful riptide of current opinion, laid-back is in; uptight is out. Tolerant is in; dogmatic is out. Enlightened is in; yesterday is out. Thus the brilliance of those ads. But this goes way beyond computers. It shapes our theology, our politics, our values. It is shaping you more than you know.

Think about what you choose to wear—is it *really* only because you like it? Don't you also hope that others will think certain things about you—that you are rugged, or sexy, or environmentally conscious, or cool? A few years ago Toms shoes were the craze. The founder had a great idea—make an eco-friendly shoe and build a movement around it by giving a free pair to an underprivileged child somewhere in the world every time a pair of Toms was bought by a consumer. The shoes became a huge hit on college campuses. They also had no arch support, looked like a potato sack, and made your feet smell like a sewer in about a week. (My friends who wore Toms said they couldn't take them off in public settings because of the stench.) But the shoes sure made a statement about your socially conscious consumer choices. Very, very "in."

Except—Jesus said when we do our acts of social good, we're not supposed to let anyone know about them. "But when you give to the needy, do not let your left hand know what your right hand is doing, so that your giving may be in secret." Hmm. What is really at work here?

According to Jesus, anyone wanting to pursue a true life, anyone wanting to live with integrity and authenticity, has to be honest about his motives. Anything less is a farce. This is no cause for shame. But it does beg a little humility, and honesty. Our fig leaf is not quite as noble as we thought. I am about to order a pair of shoes online. I know what I like. I also know what my peers would think was cool and, *more* important, what would invite quite a bit of grief. What's really influencing me? The scripture says, "The fear of man is a snare." The fear of man is a terrible motive for the things we choose to say or not say, wear or not wear, the politics we hold, the theology we embrace or reject.

Let me push a little further into this. How about personality? Most people don't realize that what we call our personality has some very profound motives behind it.

Every child is born into this world without a deep and enduring confidence in the goodness of God. That's part of what we got from Adam and Eve. We are born into this world doubting God—and then things happen. We are wounded. We are disappointed. Shame takes hold. On other occasions, we are rewarded, we are noticed, we fit in. Convictions begin to form within us. When it comes to the wounding and the shame, we say, *I know how to make sure that never happens again. I will be shy; I will be friendly; I'll keep my mouth shut; I'll be funny all the time.* When it comes to getting rewarded, noticed, invited "in," we say, *I know how to make sure that happens, too—I'll be smart, athletic, pretty, spiritual.* On and on it goes. These things are constructed over time, and they operate as what we call our personality, our approach to life. Friends, your personality is *designed* to accomplish exactly what it's accomplishing: avoid shame, get a little applause.

I can be a very driven man; I set very high standards; I push myself hard. There are certain "rewards" that come along with this way of living: I get a lot done, I can be successful. But that drivenness that the world so often rewards is really quite godless. The motive is horrible. It is born from two sources: an early childhood wound of abandonment, and a very early resolution that said, *Fine. I'll go it alone.* It's a combination of woundedness and sin. It looks fine on the outside, but inside, this cup needs a good bit of scrubbing.

A guy I worked with always loved to pronounce his words very carefully, sometimes using a British pronunciation (though he was from Los Angeles). It had nothing to do with diction; he *desperately* wanted to be seen as intelligent. Another colleague would always ask, "How *are* you?" But the truth is, he did it so that you would ask *him* how he was; he wanted to be asked. A third guy in the office was constantly dropping the ball on his projects; he would say, "I'm just not an organized person." How convenient—it required everyone else to cover for him. How lovely! You get to live irresponsibly and make others carry the load. Friends, there is always a motive to the way we're living.

We say we're not comfortable in social settings; I want to ask, "And how does that work for you?" Does it allow you to forgo the hard work of learning to relate to other people, to make conversation that engages them? How convenient.

Take as another example issues of masculinity and femininity. Sometimes I'll run into guys who say they "don't go for all that outdoor stuff." That's fine; you don't have be a lumberjack to be a man. The central issue of masculinity is courage; courage can express itself in the city as much as in the outdoors. However, I want to push into this dismissal a bit and ask why? Why is it *really* that you are not "into" outdoor stuff? You see, every man has a very deep and powerful commitment never, ever to place himself in a situation where he might be exposed. The outdoors exposes us; it tests us. Avoiding it is safe. How convenient. (On the other hand, guys who always have to have Carhartts on or cowboys boots—what's *that* about?) Do you see how the issue of motive runs deeper than, "I'm into this and you're into that"?

In a similar fashion, women often tell me, "I'm not really into all that women's stuff—dresses, makeup, jewelry." That's okay—lots of women are more "tomboyish" or athletic; perhaps they are into engineering; maybe they just like blue jeans. That's fine; femininity expresses itself in many ways. But may we push into that a little bit? Have you ever asked what's behind that? *Why* don't you want to be seen as feminine? Might it be that you fear you are not, so why bother trying? Might it be that you don't want to draw the attention of men? And why is that? How is that safer for you? (And those of you gals who won't leave the house without your makeup on—what's *that* about?)

Friends, I hope you begin to see that we all have an approach to life, and we think our approach entirely justified. It has never even occurred to most of us that our *personality* is a reflection of our holiness! But listen to this definition St. Paul offers in the Book of Romans:

Everything that does not come from faith is sin. (14:23)

Well, now—that boils things down pretty quickly. Sin is not primarily an issue of behavior; it isn't an issue of correct doctrine. It is an issue of *motive*. Whatever isn't born out of deep confidence in God is sin. That includes our personality and our approach to life.

Some friends invite you to a party; you decline, explaining that you're busy. But the truth is you're really uncomfortable at parties. The issue is fear. That's not faith; it's a self-protective move on your part. And it isn't loving, it isn't holy. On the other hand, some of you cannot bear to be left out of a party; you always make sure somehow or other to get yourself included. Why? You fear rejection; you need to be affirmed by others' interest in you. That's not faith, either; it's controlling. It is also a self-protective move on your part, just as unholy.

Everything we do has a motive behind it. This is such a helpful category. It will be the dawning of a new day for us when we can simply accept Jesus' offer of genuine integrity by looking at our motives. Begin to be honest about your motives. There's no shame, no condemnation; everything is covered by the grace of Christ. (More on that in a bit.) So let's go ahead and put it all on the table. Just begin to be honest about your motives. "This is really what's fueling me. This is why I say this or don't say that. This is why I eat this or don't eat that. This is why I go to church. This is why I pray. This is what is motivating me." And then begin to choose otherwise.

Begin to *choose* according to motive. This is where genuine goodness is lived out; this is the real deal. The sense of personal integrity that it will give you will be profound, absolutely profound. What a relief to operate not out of fear, but out of faith; not out of self-protection, but out of love. Oh, the joy of it! Once you begin to taste it, the old ways become less and less attractive. You find yourself saying, *I just don't want to live that life anymore. I want the real thing. I want holiness. I want the real deal.* So David prays,

> Create in me a pure heart, O God, and renew a steadfast spirit within me. (Psalm 51:10)

CHAPTER FIVE

A QUESTION

Let me pause at this point and ask you a question: What are you repenting of? I mean, right now, this week, what is it that you are repenting of these days?

If you don't have a ready answer, how can you be taking holiness seriously?

If your answer focuses on something external, what about the matters of the heart behind it?

It's worth a pause.

CHAPTER SIX

By Way of Contrast

I remember sitting in a church service several years ago while the congregation sang a worship song about holiness. It's a beautiful song that includes these lines: "Refiner's fire, my heart's one desire, is to be holy."[2]

I found myself squirming; I just couldn't sing the song with integrity. My heart's *one* desire? I don't think it's even on the top-ten list. I want life; I want love; I want beauty, joy, laughter, friendship, adventure. I want happiness. I simply didn't understand the connection between holiness and any of that. I find I'm not alone—I mean, really, is holiness something you and your friends talk about on a regular basis? With longing? Who was the last person who came to you and asked, "I really hunger and thirst for holiness—can you help me?"

---

2. "Refiner's Fire," Brian Doerksen.

We don't understand the link between holiness and the life we long for.

So let's come back to our conversation about the restoration of our humanity:

> Long before he laid down earth's foundations, [God] had us in mind, had settled on us as the focus of his love, to be made whole and holy by his love. Long, long ago he decided to adopt us into his family through Jesus Christ. (What pleasure he took in planning this!) He wanted us to enter into the celebration of his lavish gift-giving by the hand of his beloved Son. Because of the sacrifice of the Messiah, his blood poured out on the altar of the Cross, we're a free people—free of penalties and punishments chalked up by all our misdeeds. And not just barely free, either. Abundantly free! He thought of everything, provided for everything we could possibly need, letting us in on the plans he took such delight in making. He set it all out before us in Christ, a long-range plan in which everything would be brought together and summed up in him, everything in deepest heaven, everything on planet earth. It's in Christ that we find out who we are and what we are living for. Long before we first heard of Christ and got our hopes up, he had his eye on us, had designs on us for glorious living, part of the overall purpose he is working out in everything and everyone. (Ephesians 1:4–12 TM)

We were created for life, love, beauty, joy, laughter, friendship, adventure. These are the very things God wants for us. But we cannot find that life, let alone sustain it, until we are restored as men and women. The more I get to know Jesus, the more he changes my understanding of what holiness is all about. And the more I see him operate, the more I am captured by the beauty of his life. Now, in our search for the beauty of holiness, we are going to have to get a few things out of the way. Sometimes a good contrast helps us to see things more clearly.

TECHNICAL RULE-KEEPING

"You're hopeless, you religion scholars, you Pharisees! Frauds! Your lives are roadblocks to God's kingdom. You refuse to enter, and won't let anyone else in either. You're hopeless, you religion scholars and Pharisees! Frauds! You go halfway around the world to make a convert, but once you get him you make him into a replica of yourselves, double-damned. You're hopeless! What arrogant stupidity! You say, 'If someone makes a promise with his fingers crossed, that's nothing; but if he swears with his hand on the Bible, that's serious.' What ignorance! Does the leather on the Bible carry more weight than the skin on your hands? And what about this piece of trivia: 'If you shake hands on a promise, that's nothing; but if you raise your hand that God is your witness, that's serious'? What ridiculous hairsplitting! What difference does it make whether you shake hands or raise hands? A promise is a promise. What difference does it make if you make your promise inside or outside a house of worship? A promise is a promise. God is present, watching and holding you to account regardless." (Matthew 23:13–20 TM)

You can learn a lot about God by paying close attention to what gets Jesus mad. He's a pretty composed fellow most of the time (which in itself is just amazing, given how he was treated). So when he starts in with the "woe to you" rants, you know something has touched a nerve. In this case, it is religious "technical rule-keeping."

My son was applying to a Christian college this fall. Part of the process involved writing a few essays. One that the school required was an essay on "Why is keeping the rules important?" You have got to be kidding me—this is the test of a true follower of Christ? What does this say about church culture? Wouldn't a far more valuable essay be "Why is loving Jesus the most important thing a person can give his life to?" After all, "Love God" is the first commandment. What's with the obsession with rule-keeping? Was Jesus obsessed with that?

He broke their rules concerning the Sabbath.

He broke their rules about who could teach.

He broke their rules concerning "ceremonial cleansing."

He broke their rules about whom you could eat with, even whom you could touch.

He broke the rules about relating to single women.

Many times over.

In fact, his freedom was so disruptive that the religious elders decided they'd better kill him before he infected the nation with it. So Jesus must have a different understanding of holiness than technical rule-keeping.

Let's take the speed limit as an example. Does God expect you to drive the speed limit? The moralist says, "Absolutely. Every time. Without exception." But is that God's view?

For many years now, Christians have been smuggling Bibles into countries where it is illegal to possess a Bible. At the risk of imprisonment, torture, and even possible execution, devout followers of Jesus have systematically and with careful planning broken the law. Churches back home have supported them. Are you going to say that's a sin? The reason I bring it up is that the technical moralists—who fill many a pew, I might add—would say that breaking the speed limit is a sin because government laws are always obeyed. Well, then, what about smuggling Bibles? Or simply sharing Christ—there are countries where that is breaking the law. Do you obey the government, or are there higher laws that a Christian lives by?

> Then the high priest and all his associates, who were members of the party of the Sadducees, were filled with jealousy. They arrested the apostles and put them in the public jail. But during the night an angel of the Lord opened the doors of the jail and brought them out. "Go, stand in the temple courts," he said, "and tell the people the full message of this new life." At daybreak they entered the temple courts, as they had been told, and began to teach the people . . . At that, the captain went with his officers and brought the apostles. They did not use force, because they feared that the people would stone them. Having brought the apostles, they made them appear before the Sanhedrin to be questioned by the high priest. "We gave you strict orders not to teach in this name," he said. "Yet you have filled Jerusalem with your teaching and are determined to make us guilty of this man's blood." Peter and the other apostles replied: "We must obey God rather than men!" (Acts 5:17–29 TM)

There you have it: The apostles were lawbreakers. But they were very holy men. Blind technical obedience to rules and laws is obviously therefore *not* holiness.

So let's come back to the speed limit. If your child has stopped breathing, and you are racing to get her to the hospital, it is ridiculous to suggest you drive the speed limit. Of course you drive carefully, but carefully in this case also includes *quickly*. How preposterous to suggest that breaking the speed limit is a sin.

On the other hand, let's say you are driving through a neighborhood where the speed limit is thirty-five miles per hour. Legally, you can go thirty-five. However, *you* know from experience that up ahead is the house where most of the kids on the block hang out. They're always up to some shenanigans or other, and it's pretty common for one of them to dash out unexpectedly into the street after a skateboard or basketball. The right thing to do is to slow down. If you maintain thirty-five miles per hour, you may be keeping the letter of the law but you are violating the spirit of it. Which brings us to a very, very important point: God cares far more that we keep the spirit of the law than the letter of it.

The *purpose* of traffic regulations is the protection of human life and property. Are you driving in a manner in which life and property are protected? Then you've kept the law. The Pharisee who drives thirty-five miles per hour past the house where children are playing says, "But I have kept the letter of the law." Jesus is not impressed. On the other hand, let's say you are cruising down some lost highway in the Nevada desert. It is a glorious afternoon. No one ahead, no one behind. Do you have to follow the speed limit? Nope. Everything is protected, nothing's at stake; you can fulfill the *spirit* of the law without observing the letter, just as you can break the spirit of the law even though you keep the letter. Technical rule-keeping is not holiness.

But that is a pretty marshmallow example. Let's turn our attention to something far more urgent: sex.

After a number of years counseling students from Christian colleges, I am heartbroken by what passes for sexual integrity right now. The idea that has crept in (and you can understand why) goes basically like this: Everything but penetration. You can do everything but "have sex" and you're okay. Groping. Body humping. Even oral sex. (If this shocks you, I'm sorry, but it's true—this is the unspoken sexual ethic of a number of our Christian young people.) This is the poison of "technical morality." By keeping the letter of the law—"we didn't *do it*, we didn't 'have sex'"—they think they've kept the law. But hold on a second. How does that line up with "If you look at a woman to lust after her, you have committed adultery." I'm thinking if the two participants have most of their clothes off, they're probably well across that line; they are well past adultery of the heart.

Technical rule-keeping is a choice practice in many

churches. Yet it ignores the deeper issues—the question of motives, and the radical difference between the spirit of the law and the letter of the law. I believe there is an enormous amount of freedom for the sons and daughters of God. We are freed from the crushing burden of technical morality. But it doesn't mean all standards have been thrown to the wind. Far from it. We are ruled now by higher laws and, always, by the law of love.

SELECTIVE MORALITY

"Woe to you, teachers of the law and Pharisees, you hypocrites! You give a tenth of your spices—mint, dill and cumin. But you have neglected the more important matters of the law—justice, mercy and faithfulness. You should have practiced the latter, without neglecting the former. You blind guides! You strain out a gnat but swallow a camel." (Matthew 23:23–24)

Before we uncover the jewel in this passage, can we pause and enjoy Jesus himself for a moment? In the midst of his passionate, thundering tirade, Jesus has such a facility with words. What a turn of a phrase—straining gnats and swallowing camels. It is colorful, undeniable, swift, and devastating. Wow! Jesus is brilliant.

I knew a man who was fired from his job at a Christian high school because one of the church elders saw him purchasing cigarettes at the local grocery store. They canned him, even though he was the best teacher they had. Now, first off, the Bible does not prohibit smoking. But this has become a favorite of the technical morality police in certain churches. What is even more diabolical about the story is the pleasure these Pharisees had in firing the young teacher. Their judgment was swift and severe; their self-righteous smugness was far sicker than this guy smoking a cigarette. Jesus calls this straining gnats but swallowing camels.

The poison of technical rule-keeping is that it shifts the focus from serious issues to ridiculous peccadilloes, thus allowing the legalist to live what he believes is a "righteous life" when in fact he is failing at the very things God majors in. Take as an example a man who hates his wife; he resents her. But he has never committed adultery; he is "faithful" to her. He prides himself on his selective morality—keeping the letter of the law while ignoring massive problems in his heart. Is this holiness?

Ask yourself what it would take for a person to get fired from your church, your Christian school or ministry. What is your church's understanding of holiness? What are the categories they are thinking in? It is a very revealing test. The scriptures say that the way you treat people is a little more important than whether you smoke, for heaven's sake. Pride and arrogance are far more serious issues than swearing; idolatry and hatred are far more serious than how fast you drive.

In fact, holiness isn't even the same thing as morality. You can be a moral person and not love God. You can keep the laws and hate your neighbor. Jesus is not trying to produce Pharisees; he is trying to restore our humanity by giving us the beauty of his holiness, make us whole and holy by his love.

Blurring Moral Differences

Next Jesus let fly on the cities where he had worked the hardest but whose people had responded the least, shrugging their shoulders and going their own way. "Doom to you, Chorazin! Doom, Bethsaida! If Tyre and Sidon had seen half of the powerful miracles you have seen, they would have been on their knees in a minute. At Judgment Day they'll get off easy compared to you. And Capernaum! With all your peacock strutting, you are going to end up in the abyss. If the people of Sodom had had your chances, the city would still be around. At Judgment Day they'll get off easy compared to you." (Matthew 11:20–24 TM)

Wait a second—what did he just say? That come Judgment Day, things are going to be more severe for certain people than they will be for others? That some crimes are more serious than others? Of course. You don't really believe that the kid who skips algebra class is the moral peer of Osama bin Laden, do you?

I bring this up because something really pernicious has sneaked into the Church's understanding of holiness and sin. To be fair, I think the mistake began with good intent; then it morphed into something destructive. We understood sin to be a serious matter; we also understood that any sin separates us from God:

> What shall we conclude then? Are we any better? Not at all! We have already made the charge that Jews and Gentiles alike are all under sin. As it is written: "There is no one righteous, not even one ... There is no difference, for all have sinned and fall short of the glory of God ..." (Romans 3)

If this weren't true, the sacrifice of Jesus Christ would have been a very costly mistake. We all stand in need of forgiveness. That is true.

However, this idea has morphed into the popular notion that, "all sins are pretty much the same." It doesn't matter what the details are; sin is sin. I've heard that very phrase from many church leaders. Really? Sexual abuse is the same as jaywalking? I've met Bible scholars who would actually tell you yes. Jesus clearly *doesn't* agree. He felt that because the townspeople of Capernaum had seen him in person—God in the flesh—witnessed with their own eyes his life and miracles and had still rejected him, their crimes were far more serious than the homosexuality of Sodom. Whoa.

Jewish radio commentator and teacher Dennis Prager calls it "moral equivalency"—blurring moral differences, making all ethical issues equal, and therefore all sins equal. The idea is devastating for several reasons. First, I believe it has added to the sexual collapse I mentioned earlier. Good grief, if in the heat of passion you believe "a sin's a sin" and this is really no different from cheating on a test, and what the heck, you've already gone this far, you aren't going to have much reason to keep your clothes on. Confusing the weight of sins actually hurts our ability to resist temptation.

But the blurring of moral differences has also torn many a tender conscience apart. When a dear soul comes before God to repent of lying to her boss, and she believes (because she's been told) that she has done something just as awful as murdering her neighbor, she finds it very hard to receive forgiveness. She puts herself through all sorts of severity that frankly the offense simply doesn't call for.

This is not the view Jesus holds on the matter. All he

said to the woman caught in adultery was "go and sin no more." But to the cities that rejected him, he shouts a warning that it is going to be a mighty black day come the end. There are moral differences; some matters are far weightier than others.

Furthermore, you can't pursue genuine holiness if you are walking around under the crushing weight that tossing a wrapper on the sidewalk is just as bad as harboring resentment toward your parents. It's crippling; it also keeps you from focusing on what Jesus called "the weightier matters."

The idea has also had devastating consequences when it comes to our influence in public life. It has clouded many a Christian's thinking around election time. Trees are important, but not nearly as important as human life. Education is important, but not nearly as important as the sanctity of marriage. Blurring moral differences tries to make all things equal. They are not.

POPULAR "GOODNESS"

Let me try another example I think will help you here.

Last Saturday I was shopping at our local grocery store. It's one of those hip "organic/fair trade/eco-friendly" markets that are becoming popular. When I reached the checkout line, the cashier asked, "Do you have your own bags today?" I did not bring my own grocery bags. To be honest, it hadn't even crossed my mind. But in that culture, with all ears listening, I felt like a scumbag. I felt like the guy who doesn't care what his impact is in the world. I'm "that guy" who is sending the polar bear to a watery grave and chopping down the last rain forest myself.

Now, you wouldn't think that morality would ever become popular in the world, but there is a certain kind of "goodness" that is actually quite hip these days. Issues such as the size of your carbon footprint (and therefore the car you drive), where your coffee and chocolate come from, how your vegetables are grown or your fish is caught, the kind of shoes you wear—these are the causes du jour. Before I continue, let me say clearly *I think these things are important.* I don't think they are as important as other issues, but I think they are important. I do my shopping at these kinds of stores.

But what I want to point out is the softness of popular "goodness." Recycling can make you feel like "Hey, I'm a good person," while you ignore the fact that you've abandoned your children through your latest divorce. This is human nature: to find a morality that is comfortable and convenient and let it suffice for holiness. But it is not. So you ride your bike to work, or drive a hybrid car—but you have the sexual discretion of an alley cat. Yes, you gave clothing to the homeless—but you hate Republicans; you have hatred in your heart. A classic example would be the popular bumper sticker "Mean People Suck." Um...meaning you, then, who put this mean-spirited bumper sticker on your car.

And notice this—popular goodness also serves to ingratiate you to your community; it makes you look like a very "good person." But what about the goodness that *isn't* popular at all, the kind that, in fact, makes you suddenly very uncomfortable. You who are Democrats, would you be comfortable telling your Democrat friends that you are voting Republican this year because "Issues surrounding abortion are simply far more important than issues surrounding fair trade farming?" You see, we're back to issues of motive, convenience, and selective morality.

I think the culture of popular goodness has confused a lot of young people who are sincere about pursuing holiness. Buying eco-friendly shoes is just not on a scale with loving Jesus. Riding a bicycle to work is just not nearly as weighty as telling other people *about* Jesus. They are important, but a Christian has a lot more things that are far more important.

Hearing that Jesus had silenced the Sadducees, the Pharisees got together. One of them, an expert in the law, tested him

with this question: "Teacher, which is the greatest commandment in the Law?" Jesus replied: "'Love the Lord your God
with all your heart and with all your soul and with all your
mind.' This is the first and greatest commandment. And the
second is like it: 'Love your neighbor as yourself.' All the
Law and the Prophets hang on these two commandments."
(Matthew 22:34–40)

Clearly, Jesus believes that some commands are
weightier than others. So why is it that loving God isn't
one of the categories we think in when it comes to
holiness? Churches tend to think in moral categories
of "They are faithful attendees; they tithe every week;
they hold the correct doctrines; they don't [fill in the
blank—smoke, swear, go to bars, whatever]. They're
good people." But do they love God? We have churches
filled with people who don't really love God as the central mission of their lives; and yet they are faithful and
they attend, so we think, *wow, that's great, they're neat people*. But they're flunking Holiness 101.

Doubt Is Not a Virtue

One last thought as we sweep away some of the clutter
about holiness.

I don't remember the issue my friend and I were talking about—it had something to do with Christianity—but I do remember my friend's response: "Gosh, I'm not really sure," he said. And I thought it a humble and gracious posture to take. Only it's been five years now and he's still saying, "I'm not really sure." He has landed in that place. Now I see what happened. He has *chosen* doubt, a posture very attractive and honored in our day.

Doubt is "in."

Listen to how people talk (especially young adults): "I don't really know . . . I'm just sort of wrestling with things right now . . . you know, I'm not really sure . . ." And if in the rare case someone actually says what they believe, they quickly add, "but that's just the way *I* see it." As if confidence were a bad quality to have. Certainty is suspect these days. It doesn't seem "real" or "authentic." It's human to doubt. So it seems more human to express doubt than certainty. We end up embracing doubt because it feels "authentic."

Add to this guilt by association. Dogmatic people—people with an arrogant certainty—have done a lot of damage. Particularly dogmatic religious people. Good people don't want anything to do with that, and so—by a leap of logic—they don't want to be seen as having strong convictions. Certainty is not something they want to be associated with. Besides, the culture is honoring doubt right now. When the first of the *Narnia* movies came out, I was shocked to see what the screenwriters had done to the character of Peter. They took a young man C. S. Lewis portrays in the books as strong and courageous and made him doubting and uncertain. It was a total rewrite of his character, and it spoke volumes about where the world is right now. The writers did this to make Peter more "believable." Because doubt is "in."

Director Peter Jackson did the same violence to the character of Aragorn when he filmed Tolkien's trilogy *The Lord of the Rings*. In the original books, Aragorn is a strong, confident man. He is humble but not vacillating. The movie portrays him as a postmodern hero riddled with uncertainty, self-doubt, and regret. As if we can't bring ourselves to believe in the heroic anymore. It made me furious. It made me think of a quote by Alan Bloom. Referring to a fundamental assumption the postmodern makes, Bloom says:

> The true believer is the real danger. The study of history and of culture teaches that all the world was mad in the past; men always thought they were right, and that led to wars, persecutions, slavery, xenophobia, racism and chauvinism. The point is not to correct the mistakes and really be right; rather it is not to think you are right at all. (*The Closing of the American Mind*)

So doubt, masquerading as humility, has become a virtue, a prerequisite for respect. People of strong conviction are suspect. Many Christians I know have settled for a sort of laid-back doubt, believing it to be a genuine character decision; they thinks it's a virtue. Now, I appreciate the desire for humility, and the fear of being dogmatic. I think those are good concerns. But friends, conviction is not the enemy. Pride is. Arrogance is. But not conviction. As G. K. Chesterton said, "An open mind is really a mark of foolishness, like an open mouth... The object of opening the mind, as of opening the mouth, is to shut it again on something solid."

Enter Jesus (who is always so wonderfully countercultural). There is no question about his sincerity, his humility, or his graciousness. But doubt—this will be a great surprise to many people—is not something Jesus holds in high esteem.

Immediately Jesus made the disciples get into the boat and go on ahead of him to the other side, while he dismissed the crowd. After he had dismissed them, he went up on a mountainside by himself to pray. When evening came, he was there alone, but the boat was already a considerable distance from land, buffeted by the waves because the wind was against it. During the fourth watch of the night Jesus went out to them, walking on the lake. When the disciples saw him walking on the lake, they were terrified. "It's a ghost," they said, and cried out in fear. But Jesus immediately said to them: "Take courage! It is I. Don't be afraid." "Lord, if it's you," Peter replied, "tell me to come to you on the water." "Come," he said. Then Peter got down out of the boat, walked on the water and came toward Jesus. But when he saw the wind, he was afraid and, beginning to sink, cried out, "Lord, save me!" Immediately Jesus reached out his hand and caught him. "You of little faith," he said, "why did you doubt?" (Matthew 14:22–31)

Jesus doesn't commend Peter for his authenticity. "Wow, Peter, I love how true you were to your confusion and how honest you were with your doubts, sinking in the ocean. So many people will be able to relate to that." No, he rebukes him for doubting.

Now Thomas (called Didymus), one of the Twelve, was not with the disciples when Jesus came. So the other disciples told him, "We have seen the Lord!" But he said to them, "Unless I see the nail marks in his hands and put my finger where the nails were, and put my hand into his side, I will not believe it." A week later his disciples were in the house again, and Thomas was with them. Though the doors were locked, Jesus came and stood among them and said, "Peace be with you!" Then he said to Thomas, "Put your finger here; see my hands.

Reach out your hand and put it into my side. Stop doubting and believe." (John 20:24–27)

Stop doubting and believe. That's pretty clear. It used to be that being called a Doubting Thomas was a source of shame. These days it could be the name of an alternative rock band: "Doubting Thomas...cool, dude. I totally hear you."

One more observation about doubt: not only does it make you fit comfortably within the culture, but it also excuses you from having to act. If you really believed, for example, that abortion was taking an innocent life, you would be compelled to speak out about it. And boy, wouldn't *that* put you at odds with your neighbors! If you were convinced that people actually did go to hell unless they knew Christ as Savior, you would have to be far bolder about sharing your faith—and wouldn't *that* be awkward at work? So, take notice just how convenient doubt is for you. Motives are at play here, friends. So let us remember this truth: Doubt is not a virtue. Doubt is not humility. Doubt is doubt. It is unbelief. Jesus understands doubt, and he wants us to get past it, not embrace it, for heaven's sake.

I raise these examples because they reflect the times. We are urged in scripture not to let the times infect us. "Religion that God our Father accepts as pure and faultless is this: to look after orphans and widows in their distress and to keep oneself from being polluted by the world" (James 1:27). We breathe this present cultural air; we take in its assumptions. "The world" might mean our church wrapped up in technical rule-keeping and straining gnats; it might be the culture swept up in comfortable goodness and leisurely doubt.

We're after something far more genuine: the beautiful holiness of Jesus.

PART 2

THE WAY TO HOLINESS

"Courage! Take heart!
God is here, right here,
on his way to put things right
and redress all wrongs.
He's on his way! He'll save you!"

Springs of water will burst out in the wilderness,
streams flow in the desert.
Hot sands will become a cool oasis,
thirsty ground a splashing fountain.

There will be a highway
called the Holy Road.

The people God has ransomed
will come back on this road.
They'll sing as they make their way home to Zion,
unfading halos of joy encircling their heads,
welcomed home with gifts of joy and gladness
as all sorrows and sighs scurry into the night.

Isaiah 35:3–10 TM

CHAPTER SEVEN

ALL IS FORGIVEN

I had a horrible night last night.

I don't quite remember every detail of the dream I had, but it involved our family and my relationship with my sons, and the theme of it was this: I was failing terribly as a father. I awoke in the dark, but the message persisted: *You have blown it with your sons.* Like an avalanche, the data rushed in: I haven't spent enough time with them. I haven't shown them how to study the Bible. I've ignored warning signs. I missed key moments in their lives. My life has been far more about me than about them. My anger has wounded them permanently. You parents know how quickly the "facts" rush in to sentence you and how horrible it feels. I felt sick at heart.

And the feeling felt "true," as in, *It's all true and so you ought to feel terrible.*

Lying there in the dark, I decided impulsively to begin

a series of actions that would make amends: First, a sort of self-hating repentance with scoops of shame piled on. *Oh, God forgive me, what a failure I've been.* Followed by a mad rush of mental plans to try to atone for my mistakes by doing what I could to redeem things with my sons. This, too, felt very "real" and "appropriate."

Except, none of it was from God. Not the conviction, nor the repentance, nor the making amends. None of it.

The "conviction" I felt was the hot breath of hell, the accusations of the evil one. (He is, after all, called the Accuser.) The "repentance" I was being swept toward was the labyrinth of shame and self-loathing he loves to pile upon us. And the "amends" were unnecessary atonements for crimes never committed.

CONDEMNATION IS NOT CONVICTION

The name of the slough was Despond. Here, therefore, they wallowed for a time...and Christian, because of the burden that was on his back, began to sink in the mire...but I beheld in my dream, that a man came to him, whose name was Help, and asked him what he did there. Then, said he, Give me thine hand: so he gave him his hand, and he drew him out, and he set him upon sound ground...And he said unto me, "This miry slough is such a place as cannot be mended: it is the descent whither the scum and filth that attends conviction for sin doth continually run, and therefore it is called the Slough of Despond; for still, as the sinner is awakened about his lost condition, there arise in his soul many fears and doubts, and discouraging apprehensions, which all of them get together, and settle in this place: and this is the reason of the badness of this ground." (John Bunyan, *Pilgrim's Progress*)

I bring this up at this point in our search because I know the enemy is going to try to stop any real progress or breakthrough. And being the Deceiver that he is, his choice means are various forms of false conviction.

A woman I counseled years ago suffered profoundly from shame. If you were to listen to her story, you would know why. Throughout her childhood she lived under a constant artillery barrage of verbal abuse—put-downs at school, rage from both her mother and father at home. Over time the verbal assault shattered her heart and destroyed any self-worth she might have had. Shame became her "normal." In her twenties she found Christ, or he found her; she became a Christian. But the strongholds of shame continued to operate. As she began to hear messages on holiness, or as Jesus tried to show her something in her life that needed addressing, she fell immediately into shame. *I'm such a horrible person. God is mad at me. I'm a disappointment to everyone. I hate myself.* And what was worse, the shame felt legitimate, it felt as if it were coming straight from God himself. Shame masqueraded as conviction.

But the fruit of these convictions was never, ever fruitful. She felt loads more despair, more self-hatred, but there was never any lasting change, never the beautiful holiness of Jesus. And here is where you will be rescued, friends: You shall know them by their fruit (one of Jesus' favorite tests).

"Godly sorrow brings repentance that leads to salvation and leaves no regret, but worldly sorrow brings death." (2 Corinthians 7:10)

Wow! Read it again. No regret? There you have it. This will be a great help to you as you pursue genuine holiness. When it comes to looking at our failures, there are two kinds of sorrow: One brings life, the other death. One leaves no regret, the other destroys us. What I felt in the night as a father was simply crushing. The data felt "true" and the sorrow felt "true," but there was no life in them, no hope. It wasn't conviction but *condemnation*. It didn't feel like an invitation to change; it was simply and irrefutably a verdict on my life. The shame my friend felt as a woman seemed to be an appropriate hatred of her sin, but in fact it was merely self-loathing and nothing more.

Never once did it bring her closer to Christ, or closer to change. Quite the opposite. If only she knew this:

> Therefore, there is now no condemnation for those who are in Christ Jesus, because through Christ Jesus the law of the Spirit of life set me free from the law of sin and death. (Romans 8:1–2)

I cannot say strongly enough how important this will be to you. Condemnation is not from God. The voice of the Father is never condemning. Firm at times, of course, but never condemning. Rather, when God convicts us of sin, it is always with the hope and invitation to leave that sin behind.

> God's kindness leads you toward repentance. (Romans 2:4)

I know too many times how "real" the Accuser's accusations feel. Too many times have I accepted condemnation as God's conviction. The awful hook about false conviction is that you can feel as if you're hearing from God. *If I'm guilty, at least God is speaking to me.* The Church has practically enshrined this belief. Many Christians think the scriptures talk about "What a wretch I am." This has been canonized in the hymn "Amazing Grace": "Amazing grace how sweet the sound that saved a wretch like me." And yet that is not how the scriptures use the phrase! In Romans 7, Paul is talking about how awful it is to find himself wanting to do one thing but doing another; not wanting to do something and finding himself doing it:

> I do not understand what I do. For what I want to do I do not do, but what I hate I do. And if I do what I do not want to do, I agree that the law is good. As it is, it is no longer I myself who do it, but it is sin living in me. I know that nothing good lives in me, that is, in my sinful nature. For I have the desire to do what is good, but I cannot carry it out. For what I do is not the good I want to do; no, the evil I do not want to do—this I keep on doing. Now if I do what I do not want to do, it is no longer I who do it, but it is sin living in me that does it. So I find this law at work: When I want to do good, evil is right there with me. For in my inner being I delight in God's law; but I see another law at work in the members of my body, waging war against the law of my mind and making me a prisoner of the law of sin at work within my members. What a wretched man I am! (Romans 7:15–24)

Not "I am a wretch," but "how wretched is this horrible quandary I find myself in." Do you hear the difference? "How miserable I am," not "what a despicable specimen of a human being I am." Eugene Petersen gets the translation better into our modern language:

> I realize that I don't have what it takes. I can will it, but I can't do it. I decide to do good, but I don't really do it; I decide not to do bad, but then I do it anyway. My decisions, such as they are, don't result in actions. Something has gone wrong deep within me and gets the better of me every time. It happens so regularly that it's predictable. The moment I decide to do good, sin is there to trip me up. I truly delight in God's commands, but it's pretty obvious that not all of me joins in that delight. Parts of me covertly rebel, and just when I least expect it, they take charge. I've tried everything and nothing helps. I'm at the end of my rope. Is there no one who can do anything for me? Isn't that the real question? (7:18–24 TM)

"A wretch like me" isn't even in the text. Yes, Paul is at the end of his rope. Yes, something has gone wrong deep within him. But rather than turning to self-loathing and condemnation, he is moved to cry out for help.

The test is simple: Does the "conviction" or the "sorrow" cause us to run to God? Does it produce *intimacy* with Jesus? Shame never brings anybody closer to Jesus. Self-reproach or self-hatred never bring anybody closer to Jesus. Yes, sin is a mighty serious matter. God is insistent upon our transformation, you bet he is. But listen:

> Sin shall not be your master, because you are not under law,
> but under grace. (Romans 6:14)

You are not under law, but under grace. Did you hear that? How will be we set free from sin? Not by condemnation. By grace.

ALL IS FORGIVEN

Let's come back to Zacchaeus and the town harlot who crashed the party to weep at Jesus' feet. They were, both of them, very keenly aware of their failures. They knew they had fallen way short of God's goodness. And not only did they know it, but so did everyone else. So they bore the double weight of their own personal shame and the contempt of their communities. And yet, when they encountered Jesus—a man whose goodness shone like the sun—they ran *toward* him. How could it be?

They knew he was merciful. They knew they would find forgiveness.

As will you. God's promise to us is total forgiveness if we will come to him and ask for it:

> If we confess our sins he is faithful and just and will forgive us
> our sins and purify us from all unrighteousness. (1 John 1:9)

This offer is for everyone. It is for you and for me. And it is our only hope. We cannot begin to truly face our lives in the light of God's goodness until we know that we are under grace, that all is forgiven. Think of the difference between these two scenarios: Someone whom you love pulls you aside and says, "Can I talk to you about something I see in your life?" Versus this: Someone you know who doesn't even *like* you calls you into his office to say, "I need to talk to you about your life." Your internal reaction is totally different. None of us wants to be exposed; none of us runs around hoping this will happen. Remember the way we act in elevators: we hide. But in the case of love, you can face your life because you know there is no condemnation. This is how it is meant to be between us and Jesus.

Whatever it is you need to face about yourself, it has already been forgiven. You can go there because though the exposure may be painful—who wants to take a look in the mirror?—you are under grace.

I share this because it is hard to face our sin. The whole thing is booby-trapped with shame, fear, condemnation, dodging, equivocating, and all manner of false conviction. The only way through the slough of despond is this: All is forgiven. Everything. Now come to Jesus so you can get things straightened out.

CHAPTER EIGHT

What God Did for You in Jesus

God set about in Jesus Christ the restoration of humanity. Your humanity.

> God knew what he was doing from the very beginning. He decided from the outset to shape the lives of those who love him along the same lines as the life of his Son. The Son stands first in the line of humanity he restored. We see that original and intended shape of our lives there in him. After God made that decision of what his children should be like, he followed it up by calling people by name. After he called them by name, he set them on a solid basis with himself and then after getting them established, he stayed with them to the end, gloriously completing what he had begun. (Roman 8:29–30 TM)

Something absolutely wonderful has been done for you through Jesus Christ. The life you have always wanted to live is now available to you. But in order to begin to experience it—*before* we can experience it—we need a basic understanding of what has been accomplished on our behalf. Then, in the next chapter, we'll dive into how we actually embrace what has been done. What has God done for you through Jesus Christ? How did he intervene so that you might share in his goodness?

First, through the sacrifice of Jesus of Nazareth upon the cross, your sins have been completely forgiven:

This is love, not that we loved God, but that he loved us and sent his Son as an atoning sacrifice for our sins. (1 John 4:10)

In him we have redemption through his blood, the forgiveness of sins. (Ephesians 1:7)

He forgave us all our sins. (Colossians 2:13)

Through Jesus the forgiveness of sins is proclaimed to you. (Acts 13:34)

Blessed are they whose transgressions are forgiven, whose sins are covered. (Romans 4:7)

Through the sacrifice of Jesus Christ, you have been reconciled to God:

> We were reconciled to him through the death of his Son. (Romans 5:10)

> We also rejoice in God through our Lord Jesus Christ, through whom we have now received reconciliation. (Romans 5:11)

> We have peace with God through our Lord Jesus Christ. (Romans 5:1)

> All this is from God, who reconciled us to himself through Christ. (2 Corinthians 5:18)

Through the sacrifice of Jesus Christ, you are cleansed of all your sins:

> The blood of Jesus, his Son, purifies us from all sin. (1 John 1:7)

> How much more will the blood of Christ cleanse our consciences. (Hebrews 9:14)

> To him who loves us and has freed us from our sins by his blood. (Revelation 1:5)

If we confess our sins he is faithful and just and will forgive us
our sins and purify us from all unrighteousness. (1 John 1:9)

Through the sacrifice of Jesus Christ, you have been
delivered from the tyranny of that part of you in bondage
to sin:

Our old self was crucified with him...that we should no
longer be slaves to sin. (Romans 6:6)

Count yourselves dead to sin but alive to God in Christ Jesus.
(Romans 6:11)

I have been crucified with Christ. (Galatians 2:20)

Those who belong to Christ Jesus have crucified the sinful
nature. (Galatians 5:24)

Through the *resurrection* of Jesus and the coming of
the Spirit of God, you now have the life of Jesus Christ
within you:

But because of his great love for us, God, who is rich in
mercy, made us alive with Christ. (Ephesians 2:4–5)

God made you alive with Christ. (Colossians 2:13)

And just as Christ was raised from the dead by the glorious power of the Father, now we also may live new lives. (Romans 6:4)

Through Christ Jesus the law of the Spirit of life set me free from the law of sin and death. (Romans 8:2)

There is simply no greater news in heaven or on earth.

There is also no other way toward the restoration of your humanity and the incarnation of a genuine goodness within you.

Before you rush on, read back over these truths several times; let them begin to seep into your being. You are forgiven. Your sin nature—that traitor within you that continually sabotages your best intentions—has died with Jesus Christ. You have the life of Jesus living in you. Now, I know, I know. It sure doesn't *feel* that way most days. But you have to ground your life in something more reliable than experience. You begin with the truth, and then it will play itself out in your life. God set about the restoration of your humanity in Jesus Christ. First, he needed to deliver you from the power of sin and the inclination to sin, so he included you in the death of Jesus Christ. Having broken the power of sin over us—and *within* us—God needed to imbue us with a new life. So he included you in the resurrection of Jesus; he has made you alive with him; the life of Jesus Christ has been imparted into your being.

Do not look to your emotions or experience to determine whether or not this is true. You start by accepting the truth as told you by the living God. Then you will discover it playing itself out in your life. That is why Paul says this:

> Could it be any clearer? Our old way of life was nailed to the Cross with Christ, a decisive end to that sin-miserable life—no longer at sin's every beck and call! What we believe is this: If we get included in Christ's sin-conquering death, we also get included in his life-saving resurrection. We know that when Jesus was raised from the dead it was a signal of the end of death-as-the-end. Never again will death have the last word. When Jesus died, he took sin down with him, but alive he brings God down to us. From now on, think of it this way . . . You are dead to sin and alive to God. That's what Jesus did. (Romans 6:6–9 TM).

This being true, he goes on to explain:

> Therefore do not let sin reign in your mortal body so that you obey its evil desires. Do not offer the parts of your body to sin, as instruments of wickedness, but rather offer yourselves to God, as those who have been brought from

death to life; and offer the parts of your body to him as instruments of righteousness. For sin shall not be your master, because you are not under law, but under grace. (Romans 6:12–14)

What is crucial here is this: *now we have an option.* Without the cross, sin would simply rule in us and over us unchallenged. The hope of genuine goodness could never be ours. But because of the work of Christ *for* us and *in* us, we now have the possibility of living a life filled with the captivating goodness of Jesus. There are choices to be made, of course—Paul makes that clear. The joyful news is that those choices are now very real and quite possible. What an utter relief! I said it was wonderful; it is wonder-full, wonder-filled.

The old saint goes on in the next chapter of Romans to describe his own experience of coming to understand the truth of this and to embrace it for himself:

Something has gone wrong deep within me and gets the better of me every time. It happens so regularly that it's predictable. The moment I decide to do good, sin is there to trip me up. I truly delight in God's commands, but it's pretty obvious that not all of me joins in that delight. Parts of me covertly rebel, and just when I least expect it, they take charge. I've tried everything and nothing helps. I'm at the end of my rope.

Is there no one who can do anything for me? Isn't that the real question? The answer, thank God, is that Jesus Christ can and does. He acted to set things right in this life of contradictions where I want to serve God with all my heart and mind, but am pulled by the influence of sin to do something totally different. With the arrival of Jesus, the Messiah, that fateful dilemma is resolved. Those who enter into Christ's being-here-for-us no longer have to live under a continuous, low-lying black cloud. A new power is in operation. The Spirit of life in Christ, like a strong wind, has magnificently cleared the air, freeing you from a fated lifetime of brutal tyranny at the hands of sin and death. God went for the jugular when he sent his own Son. He didn't deal with the problem as something remote and unimportant. In his Son, Jesus, he personally took on the human condition, entered the disordered mess of struggling humanity in order to set it right once and for all. The law code, weakened as it always was by fractured human nature, could never have done that. And now what the law code asked for but we couldn't deliver is accomplished as we, instead of redoubling our own efforts, simply embrace what the Spirit is doing in us. Those who think they can do it on their own end up obsessed with measuring their own moral muscle but never get around to exercising it in real life. Those who trust God's action in them find that God's Spirit is in them—living and breathing God! (Romans 7:20–25; 8:1–5 TM)

Friends, no amount of exposition can add to the wonder of this. Either it is true or it is not. If it is, a whole new life has opened before you.

THE GOOD HEART

Before we move on to how this can become our experiential reality, I need to make one more thing clear: the redemptive work of Jesus Christ reaches the depths of the human heart. This is absolutely essential for us to believe. For one thing, a good part of Christendom doesn't understand that this is true; they have been told that their heart is still the disaster it was before Jesus found them. Not so.

> I will give you a new heart and put a new spirit in you; I will remove from you your heart of stone and give you a heart of flesh. And I will put my Spirit in you and move you to follow my decrees and be careful to keep my laws. (Ezekiel 36:26–27)

> He purified their hearts by faith. (Acts 15:9)

> Circumcision is circumcision of the heart, by the Spirit. (Romans 2:29)

Pursue righteousness, faith, love and peace, along with those
who call on the Lord out of a pure heart. (2 Timothy 2:22)

The goal of this command is love, which comes from a pure
heart and a good conscience and a sincere faith. (1 Timothy 1:5)

But the seed on good soil stands for those with a noble and good
heart. (Luke 8:15)

God went for the jugular when he set about our transformation in Jesus Christ. He knows the human heart is
the source of our iniquities; he knows that to leave the
heart untouched would sabotage his redemptive mission.
He promised a new heart; he has given us a new heart. If
this still sounds too good to be true, if it sounds contrary
to all you have been taught, simply insert the word *wicked*
into the New Testament verses directed toward the heart
of the Believer:

Love the Lord your God with all your [wicked] heart and with
all your soul and with all your mind and with all your strength.
(Mark 12:30)

Speak to one another with psalms, hymns and spiritual songs.
Sing and make music in your [wicked] heart to the Lord.
(Ephesians 5:19)

Whatever you do, work at it with all your [wicked] heart, as working for the Lord. (Colossians 3:23)

Pursue righteousness, faith, love and peace, along with those who call on the Lord out of a [wicked] heart. (2 Timothy 2:22)

The goal of this command is love, which comes from a [wicked] heart and a good conscience and a sincere faith. (1 Timothy 1:5)

I thank my God every time I remember you. In all my prayers for all of you, I always pray with joy because of your partnership in the gospel from the first day until now, being confident of this, that he who began a good work in you will carry it on to completion until the day of Christ Jesus. It is right for me to feel this way about all of you, since I have you in my [wicked] heart. (Philippians 1:3–7)

We have spoken freely to you, Corinthians, and opened wide our [wicked] hearts to you. We are not withholding our affection from you... open wide your [wicked] hearts also. (2 Corinthians 6:11–13)

How ridiculous it is to hold on to the idea that the heart touched by Jesus Christ remains wicked. God has given you a new heart. If you do not know this or believe it, how will you ever find genuine goodness, holiness that flows from the inside out? Remember, Jesus is not impressed with external rule-keeping; he wants holiness that flows from our heart.

Yes, we still need to make choices; we still need to resist what the scriptures call the "sin nature" within us. But we are never told to crucify our hearts. The only road to holiness is to know that we have died with Christ to sin; that the deepest, truest part of us doesn't want it. What a relief. When some foul thought or desire hits us, instead of battling for hours and days in anguish, we simply get to say, "No, I don't want that. That is a lie. My heart is circumcised unto God." If you *don't* believe this, then you'll end up making agreements with whatever the Deceiver and Tempter is throwing at you. If you believe your heart is wicked, then you're going to come under incredible shame and struggle and condemnation. If you believe you want to sin, then you're going to have a mighty rough time overcoming it.

With the arrival of Jesus, the Messiah, that fateful dilemma is resolved. Those who enter into Christ's being-here-for-us no longer have to live under a continuous, low-lying black cloud. A new power is in operation. The Spirit of life in Christ, like a strong wind, has magnificently cleared the air, freeing you from a fated lifetime of brutal tyranny at the hands of sin and death. (Romans 8:1–2 TM)

What God did *for* you and *in* you through Jesus Christ gives you an option. As his life takes deeper hold of us, as we walk more fully in all that has been accomplished, we can know for ourselves the utter relief of holiness. It begins by accepting the truth.

CHAPTER NINE

Choosing the Way of Holiness

We've lived in Colorado now for more than twenty years, but I've never really learned to snowboard. I mean, I've tried. But it was always a messy, hazardous, hesitant affair. Like a dog on roller skates. There wasn't a lot of joy in it for me. I was tense, apprehensive. My basic problem was this: I couldn't get myself to commit, to lean into it. You have to lean forward; you have to lean down slope. If you fight that, you end up constantly battling gravity and balance and the downward pull of things. The good riders just go for it—they commit, they lean into it, and off they go. Then comes the joy. I've never known that joy.

I've watched friends who are surfers, and it's the same dynamic. There is a moment when you have to commit; you have to go with the wave or not. Yes, there is some paddling on your part, but when the wave picks you up, your choice is to let it, to go with it, to accept its power and let it hurl you forward. You don't create the wave; the power is utterly beyond you. Once it has you in its mighty grip, your part is to *cooperate*. Then the beauty comes.

Holiness works the same way.

What I mean is this: The power is not ours. The power comes from God, from the presence of the living Jesus Christ inside us. He is the wave. If we think we have to paddle fast enough to create the entire experience, we will end up frustrated and exhausted from all the striving. The name for that is Religion. God offers something far better: "Let me be the wave."

> Therefore, my dear friends, as you have always obeyed—not only in my presence, but now much more in my absence— continue to work out your salvation with fear and trembling, *for it is God who works in you to will and to act according to his good purpose.* (Philippians 2:12–13, emphasis mine).

God is working within you in order to make this possible. With that in mind, I want to describe to you how you can "cooperate." There *is* a process, and you do have a role. It is a process in which we can cooperate, one that needs our cooperation. But you have to begin with the perspective that this is a process that God is committed to. Before I describe some of the process, let me say that nothing beats this simple prayer:

Jesus, give me your holiness.

That's what it's all about. In the day to day, when I need it most, this is what I find myself praying: *Jesus, give me your holiness*. Friends, he *wants* to give you his holiness. Receiving it begins with *asking* for it. There's more to it than that, but it's never *other* than that. Our journey to holiness is the process whereby we receive more and more of the holiness of Jesus Christ, into more and more of our being.

Let me offer a few thoughts in the direction of experiencing the power of his work for you. There are some simple practices that will enable you to receive it more fully. For one thing, you will want to read through the scriptures I listed in the last chapter—often. Sometimes daily; certainly weekly. Whenever I start a new journal, I paste those scriptures at the beginning, so that they are always with me. Sure, I forget, and I wander, and then I get desperate, and return to them. The crucial thing is for the truth of this to take deep root in our being. For as Jesus explained,

> "If you stick with this, living out what I tell you, you are my disciples for sure. *Then* you will experience for yourselves the truth, and the truth will free you." (John 8:31–32 TM)

The Greek word used here for "stick with this" is *meno*. It means to remain, to abide; to tarry; not to depart; to continue to be present. Most Westerners have an approach to understanding that goes something like this: We hear an insight explained, we hear a fact, and we acknowledge it as it passes through our minds. Then we move on. It is an approach that has been shaped profoundly by the evening news: we watch, we move on. That is the *opposite* of what Jesus is explaining here. The idea of "continuing" in his word is a deep abiding. It implies far more than, "Sure, I read that. It was awesome." "If you stick with this," he says, "if you continue, tarry, abide in, linger with" the truth, then—and *only* then—it will set you free.

So, you'll want to "hang out" with these truths, marinate in them. Read them once a day for a month.

Embracing the Work for Yourself

Then comes the process of *embracing* the Work of Christ. (By the way, this is how most of the New Testament epistles are laid out: First the truth is given, explained, and illustrated. Then, in the second half of the book, the application is laid out. You've got to know the truth and understand it before you can experience it.)

I long to embrace the work of Christ more fully. I long to let it have its full intended effect in me. After all, God set about my restoration in Jesus Christ, so I want to receive it as fully as possible and let it have its restoring effect in me. Therefore this is a portion of what I pray every morning (as in, every single day of the week):

Father, thank you for sending Jesus. I receive him, and all his life and all his work that you provided for me. Thank you for including me in Christ, for forgiving me my sins, granting me his righteousness, for making me complete in him. Thank you for making me alive with Christ, raising me with him, seating me with him at your right hand, establishing me in his authority and anointing me with your Spirit and your love. I receive it with thanks, and I give it total claim to my body, soul and spirit, my heart, mind, and will.

Jesus, thank you for coming to ransom me with your own life. I love you, worship you, trust you. I give myself over to you now—my spirit, soul, and body; my heart, mind, and will—to be one with you in all things. I sincerely receive all the work and triumph of your cross, death, blood, and sacrifice for me, through which my every sin is atoned for, I am ransomed and delivered from the kingdom of darkness, my sin nature is removed, my heart is circumcised unto God, and every claim being made against me is disarmed. I now take my place in your cross and death this morning, dying with you to sin, to my flesh, to this world, and to the evil one and his kingdom. I take up the cross and crucify my flesh with all its pride, arrogance, unbelief, and idolatry; I crucify the self-life, all self-saving and self-securing. I put off the old man. I ask you God to apply to me the fullness of the cross, death, blood, and sacrifice of Jesus Christ. I receive it with thanks and give it total claim to my spirit, soul, and body; my heart, mind, and will.

Jesus, I also sincerely receive you as my life, my holiness, and I receive all the work and triumph of your resurrection, through which you have conquered sin, death, and judgment. Death has no mastery over you, nor does any foul thing. And I have been raised with you to a new life, to live your life—dead to sin and alive to God. I now take my place in your resurrection and in your life, through which I am saved by your life, I reign in life through your life. I give my life to you today to live your life, and I receive your life—your joy, love, hope, and faith; your union with our Father; your wisdom, understanding, and discernment; your courage and power; your holiness, integrity, and trueness in all things. I put on the new man. I ask you God to apply to me the fullness of the life and resurrection of Jesus Christ. I receive it with thanks and give it total claim to my spirit, soul, and body, my heart, mind, and will.

Jesus, I also sincerely receive you as my authority, rule, and dominion, my everlasting victory against Satan and his kingdom, and my authority to bring your kingdom at all times and in every way. I receive all the work and triumph of your Ascension, whereby Satan is judged and cast him down, all authority in heaven and on earth has been given to you, and I have been given fullness in you, in your authority and in your throne. I take my place now in your authority

and in your throne, whereby I have been raised with you to the right
hand of the Father and established in your authority. I give my life to
you to reign with you. I now bring the authority, rule and dominion
of the Lord Jesus Christ over my life today—over my spirit, soul, and
body, over my heart, mind, and will.[3]

What a fabulous way to begin the day. As you make a practice of this—or something like it—the work of Christ becomes more and more a part of you. From there, you can begin to experience it.

YOU HAVE A CHOICE

Personally, I find one of the most startling things Jesus says tucked away at the end of the fourteenth chapter of John. He is preparing his closest friends (and soon-to-be-successors) for his departure. They still don't believe or don't *want* to believe he's leaving. Here is what Jesus says to them (and to us):

Do not let your hearts be troubled and do not be afraid. (John 14:27)

---

3. This is a portion of the "Daily Prayer," which you will find in the back of this book. Many people report great results from using it on a regular basis.

Wait—do not *let* your heart be troubled? I thought to myself, *We have a choice? We* let *our hearts be troubled?* I've always assumed it was the other way around—that trouble strikes in some form or other, and our hearts simply respond by being troubled. I'll bet this is how you look at it, too. Trouble descends upon you: your house is robbed, your daughter gets pregnant, you lose your job. In that moment are you thinking, *This doesn't have to take me out. I'm not going to let my heart be troubled.* No way. We think "troubled heart" is unavoidable, appropriate even. But Jesus is talking about his coming torture, his death, and, following that, his departure from them. On a scale of personal crises, this is a ten. Yet he says, don't let your hearts be troubled.

Friends, this is important.

You have a say in what your heart gives way to.

How much truer this is when it comes to choosing goodness. You have a say in what your heart gives way to. Having been struck with the idea that it is up to *me* whether I let my heart be troubled or not, I started flipping through other passages talking about what we do with our inner life, the life of our heart. I was stunned at the number of scriptures urging us to shepherd the life of our heart:

> Do not gloat when your enemy falls; when he stumbles, *do not let* your heart rejoice. (Proverbs 24:17)

And I thought, *Dang—we love to rejoice. We don't get to indulge this?*

Though your riches increase, *do not set* your heart on them. (Psalm 62:10)

But how subtle this is; when you get a good payday or a windfall, doesn't something in you say, *Now we're okay; now we're gonna be fine.* This is wrong?

Now then, my sons, listen to me; pay attention to what I say. *Do not let* your heart turn to [the seductress's] ways or stray into her paths. (Proverbs 7:24–25)

Okay, fellas, this is *huge*: I know beauty is powerful, I know it rings all kinds of bells inside you. But you can choose not to let it in. You don't have to let lust into your heart. It is not inevitable.

Do not let your hearts be troubled and do not be afraid. (John 14:27)

I repeat this because most of you think "troubled heart" equals "natural and human response to my world." Apparently not. You actually have a say in worry, fear, anxiety, and their cousins. This is huge because these

things almost always lead to some kind of false comforter/
addiction/unbelief/medication/scrambling.

> Today, if you hear his voice, *do not harden* your hearts. (Hebrews 4:7)

As in right now: something in you doesn't like the idea of having to shepherd your heart. Life is easier, so we think, when we just "let" ourselves react to life.

The point I want to make is this: God seems to think we have a choice. The Big Lie of sin is that it is *inevitable*. This feels especially true with habitual sins. When that anger sweeps over you, when that fear/lust/anxiety/rage/envy/deceitfulness/idolatry comes rushing in, it feels like it is going to have its way. And as soon as you make that agreement—*this is inevitable*—you are going to fall prey to it. But it is not inevitable. Not necessarily. *Now we have an option*, because of all Christ has done for us, and because God is at work within us. What I love about these passages is the assumption that we can shepherd our hearts; we can choose what we let in and what we don't let in; we can choose what we "go with" and what we don't "go with."

> The notion that the salvation of Jesus is a salvation from the consequences of our sins is a false, mean, low notion. The sal-

vation of Christ is a salvation from the smallest tendency or leaning to sin. It is deliverance into the pure air of God's ways of thinking and feeling. It is a salvation that makes the heart pure with the will and the choice of the heart to be pure. To such a heart, sin is disgusting. (*Unspoken Sermons*, George MacDonald)

The new model of holiness that Jesus gives us is one that flows from the inside out—from the heart. Rather than focusing on technical rule-keeping—*did I give ten percent this month, stop at yellow lights, return that pencil to work?*—we are urged to shepherd our hearts through the day.

A guy at work gets canned; something in you rejoices. You realize that in fact you hate him. *Oh, Jesus, forgive me; I renounce this hatred. Give me your holiness here, right here, toward this guy.* It's late at night, it was a horrible day, and the donuts are calling to you. Aware now of the deeper issues of the heart, you can say, *Oh, Jesus—rescue me. Forgive me for my false comforters; forgive me for turning here so many times. I reject this idol; give me your holiness here.* This is an absolutely wonderful thing. The direction of your heart is not inevitable. You have a say in it.

REPENTANCE IN THE MOMENT

Will we do it perfectly? Of course not. Friends, let's set perfection aside. We are on our way, we are being transformed, but the moment we insist on total perfection we set ourselves up for bitter disappointment. Sin shall not be our master, because we are under grace. Grace. So it might be more helpful for us to talk about what to do when we blow it.

Repent quickly. The sooner the better. For one thing, you do not want to lose your intimacy with God. For another, you know the enemy is going to jump all over you when you blow it, and you don't want to get hammered by that for days, weeks, months, years. Also, you are after freedom; the longer you wait to repent, the deeper a hold the sin gets in you. Repent quickly; it looks something like this:

First, run to God.

Father, forgive me. I'm sorry. I ask your forgiveness for [fill in the blank: this envy, that comment, the lust, my cowardice]. *Oh, forgive me, Father.*

Second, *renounce* it. If you intend to repeat the sin, your repentance is a fraud. By renouncing the sin, you summon your soul to the posture that you do not intend to repeat it. Furthermore, when you sin, you give way to forces that you do not want running pell-mell around your soul. Sin is what gives the evil one a place in our lives:

Do not sin...do not give the devil a foothold. (Ephesians 4:26–27)

You do *not* want him taking advantage of your fall. Renounce it quickly.

And Father, I renounce this. I renounce [the envy, comment, lust, cowardice]. *I renounce choosing this; I renounce giving it a place in my heart and soul. I renounce every claim I've given to the enemy through my sin. I reject this, in Jesus' name. I banish this from me. I am dead to sin, and alive to God.*

If you don't really renounce it, you're not really breaking with it; which means you're allowing for the possibility that you'll repeat it. And what kind of repentance is that? If you ignore the enemy's role in this—many Christians just want to ask forgiveness but not resist the devil—you are being naive; you are giving him the opportunity to hang around and use this against you, either through further accusation or by urging you to sin again. Did Satan take advantage of Adam and

Eve's sin? You bet he did. Don't let him take advantage of yours.

Third, practice cleansing and renewal. "If we confess our sins, he is faithful and just and will forgive us our sins and purify us from all unrighteousness" (1 John 1:9), and "May God himself, the God of peace, sanctify you through and through. May your whole spirit, soul and body be kept blameless at the coming of our Lord Jesus Christ. The one who calls you is faithful and he will do it" (1 Thessalonians 5:23–24).

> *Father, cleanse me with the blood of Jesus; wash me right here, from all of this. I plead the blood of Christ over this sin. Wash me clean; renew me. Oh, Father, sanctify me through and through right here, in this. I ask you for your holiness here, in this.*

It took me longer to explain it and longer for you to read it than it actually takes in practice. Really, you can jump straight to this in your car, in the elevator, as soon as you step out of a meeting. (But why wait? Do it silently in your heart in the meeting.) If you *practice* this—instead of, say, just resorting to self-loathing for several hours or giving way to resignation—you are going to love the freedom it brings. Absolutely love it. Friends, holiness is ours, if we ask for it, seek it, pursue it. "[F]or though a righteous man falls seven times, he rises again" (Proverbs 24:16).

Now, I realize that there are some situations where habitual sins or massive failures create something far more stubborn to deal with. We will turn there next.

CHAPTER TEN

HOLINESS IN STUBBORN PLACES

People can get pretty messed up. Even good people. Our town has certainly seen its share of scandals, which are always tragic and almost always predictable. Sometimes the fall from grace plunges the person into a pretty dark place. When the shocking news is made public, the shared reaction is typically along the lines of *How could this have happened?* It happened for many reasons, of course, but they usually include—though it is rarely named—a wacked view of holiness.

I happened to know a bit about one recent shocker and I know that, first off, this leader did *not* believe that the heart is central. He believed that the heart of the Christian remains wicked even though Christ came to dwell within. Therefore, holiness for him was all about behavior. This is partly why I said these scandals are predictable: when you neglect the sanctifying of the heart, you set yourself up for a fall. No one can discipline himself into the holiness that we need in this world, and you sure can't discipline yourself *out* of a deep dungeon. Neglect the heart and you are toast.

Second, in this man's case there were major character issues quite apart from the sexual sin. In fact, the other issues came first and paved the way for the sexual fall. The man was a narcissist, always needing to be the center of attention. His narcissism created issues with money, pride, self-absorption, and manipulation. When you introduce duplicity into your character, it allows for greater double-mindedness to follow. We think we can compartmentalize our "issues," but they bleed over into other realms. Dishonesty with your staff soon becomes dishonesty with your spouse; feelings of financial entitlement soon become feelings of sexual entitlement. But when you say to yourself, *I don't have to look at those things*, it pretty quickly becomes *I don't have to look at this, either.*

So, the heart was dismissed. He was trying to keep up an external model of holiness, but duplicity entered in. Add to that his childhood wounds. Often in these sexual falls there is some sort of early sexual experience—abuse or pornography or "experimentation"—and those experiences create a rift in the soul into which darkness loves to rush. But the minister in this case didn't believe that the primary thing God is up to is making us "whole and holy." He saw the pursuit of "wholeness" as an intrusion by secular psychology into the Christian life. He certainly didn't want to admit to or face his own brokenness. His "fall" was utterly predictable; the man was a disaster waiting to happen.

Now, I know, it's too easy to point to these public scandals. But the problem is the Church really mishandles them. After this particular fall, I heard pastors discussing it. One leader said, "Well, we're all capable of that aren't we?" All heads around the table nodded, and bang—that was the end of the discussion. There was no thinking about it, no probing, no questioning, no real consideration of how this *does* happen, so that we might understand how to prevent it or get out of it once it had happened. The classic line (repeated by many in this situation) is "We're not going to judge. We're all sinners saved by grace." That's simply not helpful. For one thing, you are far more than a sinner saved by grace. We're *not* all capable of that. Saying we are is saying that no one grows in holiness, no one gets any better, Christ hasn't transformed *any* person's life to *any* degree. Nonsense.

I don't want to pretend that the process of our transformation is easy. You already know it isn't. But I do believe we can find the genuine goodness of Jesus in our deep and lasting struggles. I believe it can happen; I've seen it happen; the scriptures promise it can happen. It will help to keep in mind that, first, it is a *process*. A process God is committed to. It is a process in which we can cooperate, a process that *needs* our cooperation. There is a way to be good again.

THREE EXAMPLES

I think it will prove helpful if we use three scenarios of deep struggle to help illustrate how we all can deal with our own struggles.

Danny married in his twenties. Around age thirty he began to surf the Internet for homosexual pornography, though he didn't know why. The inner conflict was tearing him apart, but he explored deeper until he found himself seeking out homosexual encounters at gay bars. He repented. He vowed to himself and to God that he would stop. Given the ocean of guilt and self-hatred he felt, he was certain he would never do it again. One week later, he was back at the bars looking for sex. A year later he has given up on holiness; he's just hoping he doesn't get caught. Resignation has set in, along with depression. How could this have happened? Never in his life did he think he would seek out such liaisons. After all, he is a Christian—how can this be happening? Where is the promise of a holy life?

Dawn's issue is rage. She kept a lid on it for many years, but recently it has come out, directed at her young children. Things have gotten violent on a few occasions, but so far no one outside the family knows about it. She realizes she's crossed a line in her discipline of her kids, and it scares her. But she feels trapped; if she confesses to a friend or her priest, she fears she might lose her children to social services. So the rage goes unaddressed, a monster waiting to overcome her.

Curt is drinking too much. He had issues with drugs and alcohol in high school, but left that behind when he became a Christian in his twenties—or so he thought. Now, at age forty-seven, he's turning to alcohol again to deal with the emptiness he feels inside. He never wanted to be single, never wanted to stay in his hometown. None of his dreams panned out, and he hates his job, hates his life. So he comes home, turns on the TV, and drinks himself to sleep.

How can these folks find holiness? How can we? Again, it is a process. But the way we look at our situations, and the way we understand the interplay of three forces, can make or break our hopes for real transformation.

Sin, Brokenness, Strongholds

What then? Shall we sin because we are not under law but under grace? By no means! Don't you know that when you offer yourselves to someone to obey him as slaves, you are slaves to the one whom you obey—whether you are slaves to sin, which leads to death, or to obedience, which leads to righteousness? (Romans 6:15–16)

"In your anger do not sin": Do not let the sun go down while you are still angry, and do not give the devil a foothold. (Ephesians 4:26–27)

The Spirit of the Sovereign LORD is on me, because the LORD has anointed me to preach good news to the poor. He has sent me to bind up the brokenhearted, to proclaim freedom for the captives and release from darkness for the prisoners, to proclaim the year of the LORD's favor and the day of vengeance of our God, to comfort all who mourn, and provide for those who grieve in Zion—to bestow on them a crown of beauty instead of ashes, the oil of gladness instead of mourning, and a garment of praise instead of a spirit of despair. They will be called oaks of righteousness, a planting of the LORD for the display of his splendor. (Isaiah 61:1–3)

Notice that in each of the three passages, bondage is addressed. In the Romans passage, Paul makes clear that our bondage is linked to our choices, to what we "offer ourselves" to. In Ephesians, the bondage is a direct result of letting the sun go down on unaddressed issues, giving our enemy a foothold in our lives; the bondage here is a *spiritual* stronghold. In Isaiah, bondage is linked to brokenheartedness—God is promising to bind up (heal) our brokenness and free us from captivity. The two go hand in hand. And so we see the issues here are sin, brokenness, and spiritual strongholds. If you want to be free, if you want to experience the utter relief of holiness, you need to understand the interplay of sin, brokenness, and strongholds.

Those who don't find lasting freedom are usually trying to deal with only one category.

RENOUNCING THE SIN

Danny's story is going to reveal some childhood trauma. But Danny is thirty-five now; he is an adult, and his current sins are screaming at him. I believe we need to start here. The therapeutic model wants to head straight for the trauma. We *do* need to find healing for the wounds, but we also need to deal with the sin. In most cases, this comes first. (I am describing a model that people can use wherever they are, particularly in the absence of professional help. But if you can get to a Christian counselor, by all means do so!) You have to start with what you know; you have to begin there: *Forgive me for this sin—this sexual sin, this rage, and my abusive speech to my children; forgive me my drunkenness.* You start with repentance; you start with what you know.

Again, the hope is this: God wants to sanctify us through and through:

> May God himself, the God of peace, sanctify you through and through. May your whole spirit, soul and body be kept blameless at the coming of our Lord Jesus Christ. The one who calls you is faithful and he will do it. (1 Thessalonians 5:23–24)

Freedom comes only as we bring these unsanctified and unholy places under the rule of Jesus Christ, so that he can possess these very places deeply and truly. Therefore, part of this first step involves sanctifying the place of bondage to Christ. If it's sexual, you sanctify your sexuality to Christ; if its emotional (as with rage) you sanctify your emotions; if it involves addiction you sanctify your appetite, your obsession, and your body. At the retreats we do, we walk through this process in prayer, and many people are shocked to realize that they have never taken the first, simple step of sanctifying their sexuality (or emotions, or appetites) to Jesus Christ. But if you want to be free in this place, it must come under the total, intimate, ongoing rule of God.

> Therefore do not let sin reign in your mortal body so that you obey its evil desires. Do not offer the parts of your body to sin, as instruments of wickedness, but rather *offer yourselves to God,* as those who have been brought from death to life; and *offer the parts of your body to him as instruments of righteousness.* For sin shall not be your master, because you are not under law, but under grace. (Romans 6:12–14, emphasis mine)

There is hope of freedom because of what Christ has done. Now we have an option. But we do have to stop presenting ourselves over to sin as best we can. Our choices matter. We need to renounce the ways we have presented ourselves to sin, and re-present ourselves to Christ. It is only a beginning, but this is very important.

> *Lord Jesus, forgive me. I confess I have been offering myself over to sin, and now I am its slave. I renounce it; I renounce my sins.* [Be very specific here.] *I renounce the ways I have presented* [in Danny's case] *my sexuality to sin; I renounce my sexual sins. I present my sexuality to Jesus Christ. I sanctify my sexuality to Jesus*

Christ. I present the members of my body and my sexuality as instruments of righteousness. [In Curt's case] *I renounce the ways I have presented my appetite and my drinking to sin; I renounce my sins with alcohol. I present my appetite and my drinking to Jesus Christ. I sanctify my body to Jesus Christ. May your atoning blood cover my sins and cleanse me. May your holiness possess my sexuality totally and completely.*

I am describing in this chapter a process of prayer, but let me note two things: First, your heart has to be "in it." Casual repentance equals casual results. Stay with the prayer until you feel as if all of you were cooperating. But I have found that "in the moment of temptation" sanctifying is very important, too. When you feel the urge is the very moment to sanctify, because that "part" of you is quite awake and present, and in those "live" moments, sanctifying really helps.

Now, like the iceberg, there's a whole lot more under the surface. So you invite the Holy Spirit to reveal the roots of your struggle, because we have all let the sun go down on these things, many times over months and over years, and this is what entrenches the bondage in our life. Immediate repentance is important, but you've got to go very deeply into this to get it cleaned out and healed so that you can be genuinely whole and holy, genuinely free in this area. As David prayed,

Search me, O God, and know my heart; test me and know
my anxious thoughts. See if there is any offensive way in me,
and lead me in the way everlasting. (Psalm 139:23–24)

As the Spirit reveals each layer of this, he'll show you
times in your life when there were events that helped
create the lasting bondage. Your first sexual encounter,
for example, or times when you lost your temper and
gave way to rage; those first high school parties when
you got drunk. So in Dawn's case, she'd ask the Spirit to
show her where this rage got in, and as he did, she'd pray
over each event.

> Lord Jesus forgive me—forgive me for the time I raged at my father
> when I was seventeen; forgive me for the time I raged at myself when
> I failed the math exam; forgive me for raging at my teacher as well.
> I renounce giving way to rage, I renounce the claim I gave it in my
> life. I plead the atonement of Jesus Christ here to cancel this sin and
> set me free of its every claim. I declare that if we confess our sins,
> "God is faithful to forgive us and cleanse us from all unrighteous-
> ness." (1 John 1:9)

I am *not* suggesting a "witch hunt," where you rack
your brain trying to recall every single moment you
sinned in the particular area you are struggling with. But
you cannot ignore those sins, either. Ask the Spirit of

God to search you and to reveal where the root of the sin got in. As he does, bring each event under the blood of Jesus; renounce it, renounce "presenting" yourself to this specific sin; break with it, and ask Christ to cleanse you there.

As you're walking through this, I want you to think of it as sanctifying the past. You are inviting Christ into all kinds of emotions and memories and events in your life, because you didn't invite him in at that time. We're going back to sanctify the past.

Now, there are quite often issues involving "companion sins." In Curt's life the drinking is deeply connected with *lying about* the drinking—to his family, his boss. Remember, one form of duplicity usually ushers in several others. Confess and renounce these companion sins as well. For Dawn the companion sin is control; she is a very controlling woman and that is not faith (and whatever is not from faith is sin). So she has to renounce and repent of control just as much as she does rage. These things are linked.

You will also find it helpful to renounce the "sins of your fathers." Often in these places of lasting bondage you will find that a father (or mother, or brother, or grandparent) struggled with the same issue. Dawn's father was a raging man; sexual sin has a long history in Danny's family line; Curt's grandmother was an alcoholic. The scriptures present to us the reality that sin is often passed down within a family line, and the *effects* of those sins are also passed down generation to generation (see Exodus 20:5, 34:7; Leviticus 26:39–42; Nehemiah 9:2).

Lord Jesus, I also renounce the sins of my fathers here [or my mother, my grandmother, what have you]. *I renounce their sins of rage, their sexual sins, their alcoholism. I break with the sins of my family line. I plead the blood of Christ over those sins, so that they may not have a hold on me. I renounce them and break with them utterly.*

Breaking the Stronghold

The Ephesians passage warns about spiritual strongholds created in our lives when we let "the sun go down" on something. Note that in this case that something isn't necessarily sin. Paul says, "in your anger do not sin," so anger does not equal sin. Anger can be a very appropriate reaction to life's injustices. Nonetheless, failure to *deal with* that anger (letting the sun go down on it) clearly gives our enemy an opportunity to create footholds or places of bondage in our lives. (By the way, Ephesians is a letter written to Christians; it is therefore quite clear that Christians can have demonic strongholds in their lives.)

If you let the sun go down on these unresolved issues in your life—the emotional issues, wounds, pain, *and* the sin that goes with them—you are going to create a mess for yourself down the road. And so a genuine pursuit of holiness requires going back into those places to deal with them now.

Danny was sexually abused by his brother at age seven. The fear, shame, confusion, and guilt broke his little heart. After three years his brother was caught, and the abuse stopped. You would think that, of all people, Danny would never, ever want to see the same thing happen to someone he loved. How is it that at sixteen he became an abuser himself? Why do these cycles repeat themselves so very, very frequently? Spiritual strongholds—that's why. The enemy seizes these events to create a hold in us. In Danny's case, spirits of sexual sin gained access to him *both* by the sins done against him and by his own sins.

Dawn's father had major problems with rage. She remembers as a little girl hiding in the closet for fear of her father. Now, fear is not a sin, just as anger is not necessarily sin. The issue is letting the sun go down on that fear, for many years. Curt was a "party guy" in high school. He never really saw it as a big issue, but now that he's trying to get free from it, he realizes that the loneliness and the fear of what others would think of him if he didn't party were what got the ball rolling in the first place.

Giving way to peer pressure was the first act that the sun went down on.

We begin to break the enemy's hold on us through the presence of "agreements." By this I mean places in our own hearts that have made a deep agreement with a feeling, a thought, a sentence. If you have struggled with something for years now, there are probably agreements along the lines of: *I'll never get free of this*; *I am such an $%#@*; *who cares anyway? It's too late*; and a host of others. Those are agreements and they serve as a kind of permission for the enemy to keep you in bondage. So you must break them. In addition to these, there are the agreements with the sin itself: *I am filled with rage*; *I am a drunk*; *I am gay*. They can even "feel" biblical, but, friends, you do not want to be making agreements with your sin. You are dead to sin and alive to God. You are the dwelling place of Jesus Christ. You are forgiven and dearly loved. The scriptures even say you are holy:

> Once you were alienated from God and were enemies in your minds because of your evil behavior. But now he has reconciled you by Christ's physical body through death to present you holy in his sight, without blemish and free from accusation. (Colossians 1:21–22)

Therefore, as God's chosen people, holy and dearly loved, clothe yourselves with compassion, kindness, humility, gentleness and patience. (Colossians 3:12)

And by that will, we have been made holy through the sacrifice of the body of Jesus Christ once for all. (Hebrews 10:10)

So you must break the agreements you've been making here, in this area. Some will be obvious to you; others require the presence of the Holy Spirit to reveal them.

Spirit of God search me, know me, reveal to me the agreements I have been making in this area. I renounce those agreements now. [Be very specific.] *I renounce the agreement that* [What is it? "I'll never get free? Rage is just a part of me? It's too late?"]. *I break these agreements in the name of my Lord Jesus Christ. I renounce them. I renounce every claim they have given the enemy in my life. Jesus, my Deliverer, come and break these strongholds. Set me free in this very place.*

Now, just as there are often "companion sins," there are often "companion agreements" as well. In Dawn's case, she has a deep and lasting agreement that she is on her own, that no one will protect her. The agreement is rooted in her childhood wounds (which we will get to; these need healing, too). But she must break those agreements in order to be free. In Danny's case, childhood abuse created deep strongholds of shame. A thousand suns went down on that shame, and it never ever got addressed. He has got to break agreements with shame, because now, especially given his acting out, he is suffo-cating under shame.

> *Lord Jesus, show me every companion agreement operating here. I re-nounce the agreement that I'm alone; that no one will protect me. I renounce the agreement that I am dirty and disgusting. I renounce every agreement with shame. I renounce the agreement that I can never be forgiven. Spirit, show me what to pray, reveal these agreements.*

This is how we undo that dynamic about letting the sun go down on these things and the enemy getting a foothold. Bit by bit you are recovering parts of your heart. You are taking them back from when you gave them away. This erodes the claim that you gave the enemy in your heart. Yes, terrible things may have hap-pened to us, but we are the ones who made these agree-ments, these resolutions, these vows, and we're not going to see victory in that area until we renounce them.

I will be honest—if you've given your heart over to something many times over, you've given it a good stronghold, and if it is also tangled up in issues of wounds and sin, it's going to take some time to untangle and heal this, but it is worth the work. Don't just bury it. It's worth going into those dark places and those murky waters and working through it. The blood of Jesus Christ cleanses us of everything. Everything.

Having broken the agreements and renounced the sin, we often find that we have to be quite intentional in commanding the enemy to leave. "Submit therefore to God," wrote James the brother of Jesus, "resist the devil and he will flee from you" (James 4:7). Much of what we have been doing up to this point is submitting to God, bringing these specific issues under the rule of Jesus by renouncing the sins, breaking the agreements, sanctifying these places back to the Lordship of Jesus Christ. Now comes part two of this verse: resist.

> *I bring the blood of my Lord Jesus Christ right here, in this very place. I renounce every claim I gave the evil one to my life right here, in this very place. And I bring the blood of Christ now against the strongholds and against the spirits operating here.* [Sometimes you will need to be firm and specific.] *I bring the blood of Jesus against all spirits of addiction, of alcoholism, all spirits of rage, of homosexuality* [and so on]. *I banish these enemies from my life now—from my body, my soul and my spirit. "Resist the devil and he will flee from you" (James 4:7). I resist the devil here and now and I command these spirits to flee in the name of Jesus Christ my Lord.*

Do this with the "companion issues" as well. In Curt's case, resignation is actually what allowed the drinking. So he needs to renounce giving way to resignation, repent of it, and also bring the work of Christ against every form of spiritual bondage of resignation. It came first; then came the addiction. For Dawn, it was fear—fear of her father's rage. Fear actually preceded the rage in her own life, just like it does in a frightened animal. So she needs to renounce all access she has given to fear as well. Be aware of these companion issues. Ask the Spirit to guide you. If you will stick with this, and let the Holy Spirit guide you, you can be free.

> *Lord, forgive me for giving place in my heart to resentment, to lust, to anger, to alcohol. Forgive me for giving place in my life to resignation and self-reproach and shame, to fear and doubt and control. I renounce it now. Come, Jesus Christ, and take your rightful place in my heart and in my life here. Come and set me free here, in these very places. I plead your blood over these sins and I break every hold I gave my enemy here, in the name of Jesus Christ.*

As you do this, you erode your enemy's claims to keep you in bondage.

By the way, your enemy is not going to like the fact that you are about to get free. He will try to discourage you from praying like this. He will try to distract you (the phone will ring, you'll suddenly be hungry, you feel like *do it tomorrow*). He'll try to make you feel like *this is so stupid, I can't believe I'm doing this out loud*. He's going to make you feel like *this isn't working* or *this isn't going to work; now I'm becoming one of those nuts.* Just push through all of that.

> *I bring the work of Jesus Christ once more against you* [shame, rage, fear, sexual sin, resignation, etc.] *and I command you in the name of Jesus Christ to go to the throne of Jesus Christ in his mighty name. "It is for freedom that Christ has set you free" (Galatians 5:1). I claim my freedom now in the name of Jesus Christ. Jesus, I ask you to sanctify me through and through. May my whole spirit, soul and body, be kept blameless at the coming of our Lord Jesus Christ (1 Thessalonians 5:23–24). Sanctify me through and through, in this place, in this issue.*

HEALING THE BROKENNESS

Now for the best part: the healing. God wants to make you *whole* and holy. He promises to heal the broken-hearted. So now you invite Jesus in to heal the wound, to love you in this place, to restore your soul here, to heal this memory. You invite him into your past.

Danny needs to invite Jesus into those first sexual experiences, those memories of abuse. As he does, Jesus will come there and bring his healing love.

> *Lord Jesus, I invite you into my wounds and my brokenness.* [Again, don't be vague and general; be very specific.] *Jesus, I invite you into the day I was abused. Come into my shattered heart, my shame, come into that moment in my life. I ask you to cleanse me here, to heal my broken heart and make me whole.*

Linger in this place in prayer. Listen. Pay attention. Often Jesus will bring up something necessary to your healing. For example, suddenly you feel the anger toward your abuser—Jesus is showing you that you need to forgive.

> *Jesus, I forgive my brother for abusing me. I release him from my rage and I give him over to you.*

Sometimes you'll feel the shame and self-rejection.

> *Lord Jesus, come into this shame. I renounce self-rejection. I renounce despising myself because of all that has happened. I forgive myself as well. Come and heal me.*

Sometimes you will feel the young places in your heart crying out for love or for protection.

Lord Jesus, gather the young and frightened place in my heart into your loving arms. Come and find me here, in these very places. Gather my heart into your love and make me whole.

It is important that I stop and point out that, especially here, in healing, it is usually helpful if you have someone to pray along with you—a trained counselor or minister, someone who knows a bit about healing prayer, or simply a friend who knows Jesus and wants to help you. It is not mandatory, but it can be helpful. God will bring you what you need.

As you are inviting Jesus into your wounds, what is so very beautiful is the fact that quite often—not every time, but more than you'll expect—Jesus will show you what he is doing; you will see him come. Call it seeing with your mind's eye or Christ using your imagination or seeing with the eyes of your heart or your spirit—however you want to describe it. Often you will see Christ come back into your past. He may take you by the hand and lead you out of that room. You might see him step between you and the one who wounded you, or he might simply tell you, *You are forgiven, you are safe, I love you.*

Healing doesn't necessarily have to be dramatic. Oftentimes it is very quiet. Jesus simply comes as we invite him to, and though we may not "see" him or "hear" him, he comes, and we sense a new peace or quietness in our soul. Our heart *feels* better somehow. The important thing is for us to give him permission to these wounded places, invite his healing love, and wait in prayer for him to come. Do this with each memory of wounding, with each event (ask the Holy Spirit to guide you). Often I will pray Isaiah 61 as I do this:

> *Lord Jesus, you have come to heal the brokenhearted, to proclaim freedom for the captives and release from darkness for the prisoners, to proclaim the year of the LORD's favor and the day of vengeance of our God. Come and heal my brokenness right here, Lord; free me from this captivity, release me from all darkness, bring your favor here in my soul and bring your vengeance here against my enemies. Lord, you came to comfort all who mourn, and provide for those who grieve in Zion— to bestow on them a crown of beauty instead of ashes, the oil of gladness instead of mourning, and a garment of praise instead of a spirit of despair. I ask you to do this in me—comfort me where I am hurting; bestow on me a crown of beauty instead of ashes, the oil of gladness instead of mourning, and a garment of praise instead of a spirit of despair. Come in this memory, in this wound. I receive you here.*

Many times Jesus simply says, "Let me love you." We need to open our hearts up to his love. As we do, it allows him to come to this very place. Linger there and listen; ask for the healing grace of Jesus Christ over and over again. He comes, dear friends, he comes.

GRACE

Does it always have to happen exactly in this way, in this order? Of course not.

The human soul is a place of profound mysteries. God is a person of infinite creativity. He can do this any way he wants. Sometimes he goes straight for the wound or the brokenness. Having had that healed, we find it far easier to resist the enemy and renounce our sins. Sometimes it requires binding the enemy first, simply so we can think clearly enough to do the repenting and find the healing we need. This is an outline to the process whereby we become holy in his name. Jesus will guide you. Ask him to guide you.

Do not be surprised or discouraged if you find that it takes more than one round of prayer. It didn't take you a day to get into this mess. Sometimes you'll have to pray again in a month, and then again in six months. Listen carefully: This doesn't mean that "it didn't work." Quite often Christ comes back in our lives for a deeper work of healing. Even if you're only eighteen, the sun has gone down a lot of times in your life; there's a lot of past there. But if you're fifty-eight, there's a whole lot more past to your story. So be gracious, be patient; it doesn't mean you're blowing it if Christ brings it up again. It simply means it's time for another round, and so you go back again through this exact process of repentance and deliverance and healing.

The beauty is that as you become more whole, you can become holier. And as you become holier, you can become more whole. Trying to choose one without the other I think has really brought people a great deal of distress, brought them to the conviction that no real change takes place in this life. It's not true. It's just that discipline is not enough. As my wife Stasi was saying just the other day, "You can't repent your way out of brokenness." It simply doesn't work. We repent our sins; the brokenness must be healed. Furthermore, this isn't simply about the sweet love of Jesus. You have an enemy, strongholds are real, and you must break those agreements and banish the enemy.

MAKING LEVEL PATHS

Our fathers had disciplined us for a little while as they thought best, but God disciplines us for our good that we may share in his holiness. No discipline seems pleasant at the time, but painful. Later on, however, it produces a harvest of righteousness and peace for those who have been trained by it. Therefore, strengthen your feeble arms and weak knees. Make level paths for your feet so that the limb which is lame is not put out of joint, but rather healed. (Hebrews 12: 10–12)

After a broken leg has been set, and had time to heal, it needs to be strengthened. The same is true of your soul. God urges us to make "levels paths" for ourselves, so that we can be restored. You're going to have to make some adjustments to your life if you want lasting wholeness. Danny needs to get himself out of the bar scene; he cannot hang out in those places anymore. There may be "friendships" he has to end. You must walk away from those things that trip you up, friends. Curt is going to be helped a great deal by a recovery group; he's got to stop even the littlest bit of drinking, at least for a season. Dawn needs to open up her story to a few friends who can help her; isolation is deadly. If the Internet is the problem, get a filter. If you're addicted to daytime soaps, throw out the TV. Get rid of the "triggers" in your life. Make level paths for yourself.

Choose holiness. In those hundreds of little decisions each day, choose holiness. The more you do, the more you will find yourself able to. The more we make choices that comprise our integrity, the weaker we feel and the more the enemy pours it on. However, the more we side with the Spirit in us, the stronger we feel. Over time it becomes easier to choose; our will gets stronger; we discover that in fact, we really do want goodness and nothing else.

CHAPTER ELEVEN

THE FRUIT OF HOLINESS

In all fairness, this must be said: The process of transformation can be a painful one. I don't know why we ignore this, why we don't talk about it more often. Some of those things within us that need transformation require a deep cut of the Surgeon's knife, and he typically doesn't offer anesthetics beforehand.

Holiness will cost you. It will certainly cost you the expense of laziness; there's no more coasting through life. You have to be aware now of where your heart is going on any given day, what you're allowing in and where your heart is wandering off to. That will cost you, in the sense that there's no more slacking off anymore, no more assuming your personality and your motives don't need to be looked at. You have to be vigilant to guard your heart. Frankly, the cost for this is pretty minor when you look at the benefits: there's a whole lot of "struggle" and "battle" that never have to unfold because they never get started. Besides, as you practice self-awareness and shepherding your heart, you get stronger; it begins to come naturally, and the benefits are more than worth it. But yes, it does cost—or you'd see a whole lot more people living this way.

There are higher costs. You will have to give up precious idols, and that is almost always painful. You'll be giving up your false comforters. To maintain your personal integrity will cost you relationships. It may cost you employment. Your pursuit of holiness will cost you sleepless nights—not because you're worrying, but because you're praying (fending off warfare, breaking agreements, battling some deep issues).

You will experience a higher degree of loneliness, because they are very few people who seem to want this, and so you will feel odd. You'll wonder why people aren't wrestling with the same things you're wrestling with. You'll wonder why they don't talk about the same things you talk about or want to pray about things that seem so obvious and urgent to you. You won't feel comfortable seeing the same movies your friends do, or listening to the same music, reading the same books. And so you'll experience the loneliness that Jesus lived with. But he felt it was worth it.

A genuine holiness will—if you decide to receive the

life Jesus offers you—inevitably put you in the crosshairs
of religion. Because of their love for technical morality,
large portions of the Church will be upset with your
freedom. Because of their lack of desire for holiness,
they will not want what you're offering. Jesus was in almost constant conflict with the religious, so that ought
to give you a warning—this is probably in your future as
well. Don't look for it; I'm not encouraging that. Don't
make it your mission to go change the Church. But the
conflicts will inevitably come, simply because you are
siding with Jesus. There is a cost to that as well. But
again, Jesus clearly felt that it was all worth it, everything he went through. So did his closest friends who
followed in his footsteps. So did the vast cloud of wit-
nesses down through the ages who chose holiness over
an easy life. Their shining examples ought to give us
heart!

Do you see what this means—all these pioneers who blazed
the way, all these veterans cheering us on? It means we'd
better get on with it. Strip down, start running—and never
quit! No extra spiritual fat, no parasitic sins. Keep your eyes
on Jesus, who both began and finished this race we're in.
Study how he did it. Because he never lost sight of where
he was headed—that exhilarating finish in and with God—he
could put up with anything along the way: cross, shame,

whatever. And now he's there, in the place of honor, right alongside God. When you find yourselves flagging in your faith, go over that story again, item by item, that long litany of hostility he plowed through. That will shoot adrenaline into your souls! In this all-out match against sin, others have suffered far worse than you, to say nothing of what Jesus went through—all that bloodshed! So don't feel sorry for yourselves. Or have you forgotten how good parents treat children, and that God regards you as his children? My dear child, don't shrug off God's discipline, but don't be crushed by it either. It's the child he loves that he disciplines; the child he embraces, he also corrects. God is educating you; that's why you must never drop out. He's treating you as dear children. This trouble you're in isn't punishment; it's training, the normal experience of children. Only irresponsible parents leave children to fend for themselves. Would you prefer an irresponsible God? We respect our own parents for training and not spoiling us, so why not embrace God's training so we can truly live? While we were children, our parents did what seemed best to them. But God is doing what is best for us, training us to live God's holy best. At the time, discipline isn't much fun. It always feels like it's going against the grain. Later, of course, it pays off handsomely, for it's the well-trained who find themselves mature in their relationship with God. (Hebrews 12:1–11 TM)

It does pay off handsomely. To be set free from the sins that plague us is an utter relief. It is a joy and the healing of our humanity. That alone should cause us to know that the pursuit of a deep and genuine holiness is worth whatever it costs. But perhaps we need a little encouragement at this point, a little convincing. Is holiness worth it?

THE POWER OF HOLINESS

Everyone wants to live a powerful life. Every human being wants to feel that his presence on this earth *matters*. Those devastated souls who end up taking their own lives often do so because they feel nothing is lost with their absence. They feel in fact that they are doing the world a favor by leaving the stage. Those who live with a deep, joyful satisfaction usually have found a place where their lives are doing some great good and they *know* it. We long to matter; we yearn to make a difference. What we haven't seen is the connection between our personal holiness and our impact in this world.

In chapter 2, I began our look at the captivating goodness of Jesus with two stories: his baptism and the trial in the wilderness. Notice now what happens when Jesus returns from that penetrating test of his character:

Now Jesus, full of the Holy Spirit, left the Jordan and was led by the Spirit into the wild. For forty wilderness days and nights he was tested by the Devil...Jesus returned to Galilee powerful in the Spirit. News that he was back spread through the countryside. He taught in their meeting places to everyone's acclaim and pleasure. (Luke 4:1, 14–15 TM)

Jesus returns from his testing "powerful in the Spirit," filled with the power of God. It is from *this* place the landslide begins to happen—the healings and miracles, the profound teaching, the bold-faced confrontations and the gentle rescues. All of it flows from his holiness.

You don't hear this taught much—or *modeled* much—by those who seem to have "made it" in Christian leadership. In the Church, we've come to assume that power and influence come from skill, from expertise. We live in a world that *worships* expertise. But the Kingdom of God operates on entirely different values. One life totally given over to God is far more powerful than a hundred with gifting and expertise. Look at whom Jesus chooses to change the world: fishermen, tax collectors, prostitutes.

"Remember, dear brothers and sisters, that few of you were wise in the world's eyes, or powerful, or wealthy when God called you. Instead, God deliberately chose things the world considers foolish in order to shame those who think they are wise. And he chose those who are powerless to shame those who are powerful." (1 Corinthians 1:26–27 NLT)

Now, to be clear, I'm not saying that God waits until we have reached Jesus' level of holiness to use us. If that were true, who would ever get a chance for God to use him in this world? We'd all be waiting still. Give your life to God; he'll use you.

Having said that, *of course* holiness matters. When Peter writes to husbands, urging them to "be considerate as you live with your wives, and treat them with respect," he adds a warning that at first seems unexpected in a passage on married life: "So that nothing will hinder your prayers" (1 Peter 3:7). But think of it—is God going to honor the prayers of a man seeking blessing on his business while at the same time he is being mean to his wife? Never. The principle goes way beyond husbands. Of course our prayers are limited by our sin. If you want powerful prayers, get the sin out of your life.

Before we hold one of our retreats, I can guarantee you what's coming: a thousand reasons to compromise. I'll wind up being helped by the cute girl in the store who chose not to wear a bra today. Will I choose to look or not? Will I get irritated with a team member, give way to pride over the fact that we filled the retreat, turn to self for my sense of strength? On and on it goes, like a Mardi

Gras of temptation. (This is part of the cost I mentioned earlier. It is a painful trial, and it usually lasts longer than I thought it would.) As Chinese Christian author and church leader Watchman Nee warned, the devil doesn't really care how he gets you to sin, but simply that you do—that you step out of the protection of your life in Christ. If I give way to any of these seductions, I will be compromised. I won't be nearly so powerful at the retreat. Duplicity will have entered in. I'll either be under a cloud of condemnation, or operating in the flesh, or trying to pretend I'm doing better than I truly am.

Friends, of course holiness matters. If you want to live a powerful life, you must choose holiness.

Again, I want to prevent the enemy from sneaking in a standard of perfection. The life God uses is a life *surrendered* to him. The surrender is what matters; this is what allows the powerful life of Jesus to invade ours fully. Seek a genuine holiness and you will discover the joys of knowing that your life is making a profound difference in this world—and in the one to come.

THE RESCUE OF HOLINESS

There is power to a holy life; there are also innumerable rescues waiting to be had.

A friend of mine walked into his boss's office the other day to drop off some items. He didn't realize that though his supervisor was gone for the day, the enemy was there, about to spring a trap he had set. On the desk lay an open letter. My friend "happened" to glance down and he "happened" to notice his own name in the body of the letter. Something in him said, *Whoa—this is about you. You'd better read it and see what your boss thinks of you.* The better part of his character replied, *Run. This is none of your business. Do not let curiosity compromise your standards.* I'm sorry to say he lingered; he read the letter. In it his boss vented to a colleague over some of my friend's shortcomings. The effect was devastating. My friend left feeling betrayed by his boss, and utterly compromised in his own integrity. Further anguish and devastation followed.

Holiness would have prevented the whole scenario. This supervisor should never have written the letter in the first place. My friend should never have given way to the urge to read it. If either of them had chosen holiness, the train wreck would have never happened.

Think of the devastation caused by sin on this bleeding planet. Think of the rescues that could have happened if people had chosen holiness. That little girl wouldn't have been sexually abused; she wouldn't have fallen into sexual traps as a teen; she wouldn't have struggled with her sexuality at thirty, and her marriage wouldn't have been crippled by the lack of intimacy. If he had known the way of holiness, that father wouldn't have become an alcoholic; it wouldn't have destroyed his life, his family, and his ministry. All those thousands of people who were meant to be blessed by his life would have received immeasurable blessings. On and on it goes. The ripple effect is staggering. David wouldn't have slept with Bathsheba; he wouldn't have killed Uriah; the consequences of his sin wouldn't have inflicted an entire nation. If Achan hadn't lusted after the silver and gold he took from Jericho and buried in his tent, thirty-six men wouldn't have died in the battle for Ai.

Really, now, think of it—what unspeakable tragedies could have been prevented if holiness had ruled the day?

On an intimate scale, you wouldn't be wrestling with many of the wounds you have, and the companion sins, because you wouldn't have been wounded in the first place. On a global scale, the Holocaust could have been prevented; 9/11 would have never happened, nor the bloodshed that has followed, nor the cost of many valiant lives seeking to end terrorism. The scope of sin's aftershocks is pretty staggering. If we knew just how devastating sin really was, we'd fear it the way Christians did for centuries.

Holiness *rescues us* from sin and its repercussions.

When God says, "They will neither harm nor destroy on all my holy mountain" (Isaiah 11:9), one of the reasons this will be so is because no one living there will want to sin; no one will be able to. There will be *no harm* because holiness will be their way of life. Friends, the rescues that await your embracing the way of holiness are worth the price and then some. And there are more fruits still.

Your Greatest Weapon in Warfare

No discussion of holiness is true or helpful without a healthy appreciation for how earnestly Satan wants to destroy us. Steal, kill, and destroy is how Jesus described it (see John 10:10). Satan lured Adam and Eve to compromise one single act, one slip of holiness, and from there he has brought unspeakable carnage to the human race and to the earth. Friends, he hasn't stopped his war against us. After years of ignoring this reality and paying for my ignorance (which is often in us a *chosen* naïveté), followed by decades taking up sword and shield and fighting the good fight for myself, I have come to adore something Jesus says shortly before Gethsemane and the cross. He urges us not to let our hearts be afraid. Then he says to his close companions,

"I will not speak with you much longer, for the prince of this world is coming. He has no hold on me, but the world must learn that I love the Father and that I do exactly what my Father has commanded me." (John 14:30–31)

He has no hold on me?!! Do you have any idea what a relief this would be? Just imagine for a moment if you were fortressed to all the ploys, accusations, temptations, snares, assaults, and deceptions of the enemy. What would it be like if they had no effect on you? Your life would be a joy to live.

And how is it that the enemy had no hold on Jesus? For he tried, of course, tried every angle he could possibly think of: subtle compromise, self-securing, a shortcut to the kingdom without the cross, testing God's faithfulness, and who knows all the attempts at seduction, discouragement, vengeance, fear—you name it. And none of it worked *because of* Jesus' genuine goodness, his holiness. He was untouchable. Don't you long for this?

Just the other day a young man was recounting to me a recent event from his "accountability group." A handful of young bucks from his dorm had gathered to help one another with their sexual struggles. My friend tried to explain to them that because of the healing and deliverance available in Christ, because his holiness really *can* be ours, sexual struggles aren't an issue. They were stunned, dumbfounded. "Really? You don't want to masturbate?" "Nope." After the meeting, the enemy tried to slam this young man with temptation, tried to undermine the hope for the freedom he offered the others. But because of his holiness, the wilderness trial didn't work. The enemy hasn't this hold on him anymore.

However, while having lunch with a different young man—this fellow is now in his thirties with a wife and child—the discussion turned to spiritual attack and how to win against the sometimes relentless assaults of the enemy. The issue wasn't sexuality but judgment; my friend was feeling a great deal of judgment from his family. "Judgment is very bad things to live under," I explained. "They act like curses on our life." As we spoke, I discovered that in fact my friend and his wife were indulging in a generous round of judging themselves. "When you do that—when you sin with these judgments—you are giving the enemy a claim to use judgment against you." My friend was stunned. "Nobody ever warned me about this." In order to be free from the warfare that was coming though family members, this young couple first needed to choose holiness for themselves; they needed to stop judging.

Repentance and holiness are the only way out from under spiritual attack. Otherwise, our sins give the enemy claim to continue the assault.

This isn't a book on spiritual warfare, but let me tell you that the greatest weapon you will ever have against the enemy is holiness. Warfare often works like a presidential election—they go through all your old files. Satan looks for anything he can find to use against you. He'll drudge up old sins, he'll create strongholds through ancient agreements, he'll exploit your wounds and your idolatries to ensnare you. When Jesus says, "He has no hold on me," an equally just translation goes, "He has nothing in me" (John 14:30 NASB). This is what holiness does for us: it removes the opportunities for the enemy to steal, kill, and destroy. Satan has nothing on us, in us. Oh, he'll try, of course he'll try. But if we are sanctified in this area, it will not have the power to snare us. Our holiness then goes on to rescue all that is ours, all that is meant to happen through our lives that the enemy was hoping to stop.

With apologics to Thomas Paine, I believe that *these* days we are living in are the times that try men's souls. We are entering a period of great trial upon the earth. You've seen the news; you've watched your friends suffering. The spiritual war is heating up. Wickedness is raging like a nuclear meltdown. It is going to take a supernatural life to withstand these trials. Holiness, friends, is the strength of your condition. More and more I find myself praying, *Jesus, give me your life. Give me your holiness.*

THE ALLURE OF HOLINESS

I feel I need nothing more to convince you. If what I have laid out here doesn't do it, nothing will. The fruit of holiness is worth whatever it may cost us. But allow me to add one more reason, if only because it is on my heart: choose holiness for the sake of the Gospel.

You recall Zacchaeus' reaction to Jesus: "he wanted desperately to see him" (Luke 19:3). God wants people to be desperate for Jesus; he longs for them to long for *him*. He wants folks climbing sycamores up and down the streets of this world to get a glimpse of Jesus. Don't you? I sure do. Now, God has arranged this story in such a way that it is largely through *our* lives that people get a glimpse of Jesus. So it might be good to ask yourself, *when it comes to my life, what is the Jesus they see?*

If you want to turn your children off to Jesus, ignore holiness (or choose the technical rule-keeping impostor). Be a jerk and then insist the family pray at mealtimes; let them see you lie to your boss or your aging parents and then insist you all go to church. Want to turn your neighbors off to Christianity? Let them see you yell something nasty at your dog, then head off all dressed up for Sunday morning service. It is the lack of holiness that has clouded our "witness" in this world. Thank God the opposite holds true as well: the beauty of the lives of

God's true friends is the sweetest and most winsome argument for Jesus there could ever be.

I love the people I get to work with at Ransomed
Heart. They are some of the finest people I have ever
had the honor of knowing. What joy it brings me to hear
from the folks who attend our events that it was the lives
of my friends that brought them to Jesus Christ. "I saw
the beauty of their marriage." "I saw the beauty of their
walk with God." "They were so kind to me." "They are
so filled with integrity and strength." "It was their gen-
erosity." Wow. Isn't that wonderful? Isn't that just how
it should be? I feel like David, who wrote, "As for the
saints who are in the land, they are the glorious ones in
whom is all my delight" (Psalm 16:3). We are meant to
be the glorious ones, friends.

> The LORD their God will save them on that day as the flock
> of his people. They will sparkle in his land like jewels in a
> crown. How attractive and beautiful they will be! (Zechariah
> 9:16–17)

Think again of Jesus, of his compelling goodness.
Genuine holiness is so attractive and beautiful, so allur-
ing. Which brings us back to *your life matters*. You are
meant to have a remarkable impact in this world. It flows
from your holiness, which is to say, it flows from the

amount of your life you are surrendering to the life of Jesus Christ within you.

So let me say one more time, the pursuit of a deep and genuine holiness is worth whatever it costs you. Because holiness is an utter relief. It is a joy and a healing of your creation. It will make you powerful in the Spirit, it will rescue you again and again, it will fortress you to the enemy's attacks, it will make your life a compelling argument for Jesus because it is of the same quality as his. Finally, in these last days, the saints are being sorely tested. Holiness is your strength and your safe passage through the trial. *It is worth it.*

CHAPTER TWELVE

Two Essential Motives

Hearing that Jesus had silenced the Sadducees, the Pharisees got together. One of them, an expert in the law, tested him with this question: "Teacher, which is the greatest command- ment in the Law?" Jesus replied: "'Love the Lord your God with all your heart and with all your soul and with all your mind.' This is the first and greatest commandment. And the second is like it: 'Love your neighbor as yourself.' All the Law and the Prophets hang on these two commandments." (Matthew 22:34–40)

Only Jesus could get away with this. He has just taken the entire Old Testament—the full length, breadth, diversity, and penetrating specificity of all God's commands—and boiled it down to two. Two. Given who he is, given the witness of his own shimmering goodness, he certainly has the right to do so. But perhaps we've missed the brilliance of it, and the immense kindness, too.

People have a way of complicating things. Look at what we've done to education, taxation, or marriage. We seem committed to making all things complex. The Jews of Jesus' day had so many rules and regulations it practically immobilized them. "And you experts in the law, woe to you," Jesus thundered, "because you load people down with burdens they can hardly carry, and you yourselves will not lift one finger to help them" (Luke 11:46 TM). This wasn't what God intended. The way of holiness was never meant to be a labyrinth of complexity and eventual despair.

On the other hand, people also have a tendency to intentionally cloud the issue so that we don't have to take immediate action. High standards have a way of being ignored, because we feel as though we haven't the slightest chance of meeting them. Why bother? So we let moral issues remain cloudy as a way of excusing ourselves from ever really facing them.

Jesus cuts through both when he says, "Look—it all comes down to this: Love God, love others. Practice this and you'll be fine." He's not dismissing the many wonderful instructions God has given us in his Word; he is bringing us back to the issue of *motive*. Okay. If the entire Bible comes down to these two issues, maybe we ought to focus our attention here. Maybe we ought to make this what we are about. These are our marching orders in our pursuit of holiness: we will make loving God and loving others our motives and we shall find the beauty of Jesus' holiness.

LOVING GOD

Love God with all your heart and with all your soul and with all your mind. Jesus said this was the first and greatest commandment. So let's keep this simple: Do you love God? It all starts there. Make a practice of loving God. "But how?" a friend asked. How do you love any of the people or the things that you currently love? You delight in them. You give your heart over to them. You choose them over other things and other people. They hold a special place in your heart. They get the lion's share of your time, your attention, your presence. Don't they? Then this is what we do—we give our whole heart to God. We make him the treasure of our life.

It will be a profound moral rescue. It's pretty hard to lust after someone if in that very moment you start saying, *Jesus, I love you, I love you, I love you*. It's pretty hard to hold bitterness toward someone if in that very moment you start loving God. Whatever it is we find ourselves struggling with, right then and there in that very place we practice loving God and what we find is that our heart is freed to be good again. Loving God alone will heal your humanity. It's what you were made for.

The second commandment given to Moses on Sinai is another way of coming at the whole matter:

> You shall not make for yourself an idol in the form of anything in heaven above or on the earth beneath or in the waters below. You shall not bow down to them or worship them. (Exodus 20:4–6)

It helps us to carry out the first and greatest command: love God, and do so by having no idols. What do you love more than God? What do you look to for security more than you look to God? Where do you draw your sense of identity from, more than you draw it from God? These are the things you must lay on the altar. Here is where your most earnest repentance lies. These things may not in and of themselves be bad, but if we make a son or daughter more to us than God is, we have made an idol of them, and here we must repent. So if you back into this through the doorway of idolatry, it will free your heart up to love God. Whatever you look to for security or comfort or assurance or validation, whatever you look to to make yourself feel better or to bring you pleasure over and above or quite apart from God is idolatry.

When you say, "I love God," but what you daydream about is what you are going to eat or drink tonight, you've got an issue. When you say, "I love God," but what you care about more is what *others* think about you, you've got an issue. When you say, "I know God is my provider," but all your hope and confidence is in your career, that's idolatry. It happens anytime we look to anything over God as the source of life.

So, if idolatry is the Big Issue because loving God is the first commandment, it follows that our repentance ought to be focused mostly on the idols in our lives. Whether or not we used a "cuss word" is nothing compared to the fact that we love something more than we love God. Idols always take us back to issues of the heart. *That's* where the action is; that's where real transformation takes place.

This might help: idolatry involves sacrifice, so whenever you have sacrifice, you have serious idolatry. When you have a family that is absolutely famished for the love of a father because he spends all his time at work, you have idolatry. He has made work his god; he is worshiping his work and the money or the prestige or the power that it gives him and he's sacrificing his family to get it. Whenever you find someone absolutely wrung out emotionally, spiritually, and physically, you want to ask, "Why are you sacrificing yourself here?" Watch for the sacrifice—what is being sacrificed? You can follow that trail right back to the idol.

Loving God is the centering of your existence as a human being. It's the restoration of your reason for existence. What a relief it is to love God with all your heart, soul, mind, and strength. What an utter relief. For then, every other relationship falls into place; every other desire finds its appropriate place in our life. Again, this is why mere "morality" can never substitute for true holiness. You can keep all the rules you think are important and not love God. This is where it all begins, truly loving Jesus with all your heart. Where things are out of whack, that is where our repenting needs to take place.

LOVING OTHERS

Love your neighbor, Jesus urged, as you love yourself. (Which, as C. S. Lewis pointed out, is a pretty sick command if we are to hate ourselves.) How you handle people is the second great test of your character.

Again, Jesus is cutting through both all the complexity and our dodging by helping us focus on our motives. It's pretty hard to be a racist and still love that person.

It's pretty hard to hold bitterness in your heart and still love that person. So here, too, we find a profound rescue. Wherever it is we find ourselves struggling, we begin to choose love; in our hearts we begin to reaffirm our love for this human being. I find myself wanting to get irritated and judge: *Jesus, help me love this person.* I find myself wanting to envy: *Jesus, help me love this person.* As we allow love in, it flushes an awful lot of other stuff out.

"Do not murder," the Bible says, but what about dismissal? I write people off far too quickly, and it is not good. What difference is there between dismissal and murder, really? Aren't I basically saying, "I don't want your existence—not in my orbit, not in my universe. You're gone, you're out of here." James tells us, "Don't show favorites." Maybe we don't have favorites, but we withhold praise, we withhold love, we withhold affection, we parcel it out based on all kinds of other motives than love. Most often it is based on how they are treating me, what they can do for me.

Remember, friends, your personality has motives behind it. Most of those motives are self-protection. The way you relate to people is designed to avoid rejection and win some praise. The problem is, it has nothing to do with love. None of that reflects the motive of loving God and loving others. So this is where most of our deepest repenting will take place. We repent of our self-protective ways; we repent of our manipulation in relationships.

Now, remember, Jesus did not go around simply being nice to people. This is where the idea of "loving others" has gotten turned into a "get well" card. Christians honestly and sincerely believe that being nice is what they are called to do. No, you are called to do something far more powerful than be nice; you are called to love. And what love has in mind is not "How can I keep things running smoothly here?" but rather, "What does this person truly need?" This will change everything in the way you relate to people; it will help you love them.

Every human being has a gravitational pull. Part of this is simply personality (designed to protect you) and part of it is the warfare set against you. Have you noticed this? Think about the people you know. "Every time I'm around Jack, I just want to dismiss him." Notice that everybody does this. "When I'm around Susie, I never feel permission to be serious; it always has to be light and funny." That's her pull; notice everybody acts that way toward her. "Every time I talk to Dan, I find myself wanting to comfort him; but with Tammy, I feel like I have to praise her; and yet with David, I feel like I just want to ignore him."

That's these people's "gravitational pull." It is rooted in wounds and agreements, in self-protection, and in the enemy's stronghold in their lives. Everybody has a gravitational pull.

Now, how does Jesus handle this? He never gives way to it. He never treats people according to their gravitational pull. To the leper who won't come too close, Jesus reaches right through his shame and touches him. To the Pharisees whom everyone else feared and therefore flattered, Jesus shoots straight: "You are hypocrites." When Peter was out of line, Jesus said, "You do not have God's will in mind right now." When Peter felt disqualified, Jesus said, "Feed my sheep; I reinstate you." To those who tried to flatter him, Jesus said, "What are you really after?" It is just incredible. He never treats people according to their gravitational pull. Instead, he loves them. He sees what they most need and offers that.

This "love others" command does not mean going around being nice to everyone. It means seeing through the disguises and the gravitational pull to what these people really need, and offering that.

In Closing

Love God and love others. Honestly, if you set these two *motives* before you each day, they will see you through a thousand quandaries.

When it comes to God, we simply begin to practice loving him. We make him the treasure of our heart, every day. Simply begin the day by saying, *Jesus, you are the treasure of my life. You are my treasure. You are my heart's desire. I love you. Help me to love you today.* And then we shepherd our hearts, with his help. We notice where our hearts go looking for love, or approval, for comfort or affirmation, and in those very moments we repent. *Oh, Jesus, forgive me for this idol. Cleanse me here, give me your holiness here. I renounce this idol. I choose God.* In those moments, we give our hearts over to God in fresh and deeper ways. As John ends his first epistle, "Dear children, keep yourselves from idols" (1 John 5:21).

When it comes to people, we choose the motive of love. We begin to notice their "gravitational pull" and instead of giving way to it as we always have, we choose to offer what they really need. What do they need? They may need a stern rebuke; they may need compassion and kindness. *Jesus in me, help me love this person.* This of course includes repenting of our own self-protective ways.

As I write this, I am aware how little I am able to sustain even a day of this kind of living, let alone a lifetime. Who can live like this? Exactly. Precisely. That's the right question—who in heaven's name can live like this? You know the answer. And when we allow his life to fill ours, we find that we, too, can do all things "through him who gives me strength" (Philippians 4:13). Holiness at first can feel like it's mostly will power, decision, and determination. *No, I will not go there. I will not give my heart over to that. No, I will not let that in. I will not give that a place in me.* But over time, what we find is that we do grow stronger in the life of God as his life grows stronger in us.

The hope of Christianity is that we get to live the life of Jesus. His beautiful goodness can be ours. Jesus can heal what has gone wrong inside each and every one of us. He does this by giving us *his* goodness; he imparts it to us. We get to live *his* life—that is, live each day by the power of his life within us. That's the hope: you get to live his beautiful life. To quote MacDonald once more, "There is a reality of being in which all things are easy and plain oneness, that is, with the Lord of life." God makes us whole by making us holy; he makes us holy by making us whole. Friends, the pursuit of a deep and genuine holiness is worth whatever it costs you. There is a way to be good again.

And so I find myself praying—far more than I ever have before—this simple prayer: *Jesus, give me your holiness.* I pray it in the car, at my desk, in a meeting, at the movies, waking in the morning, before sleeping at night, wherever I am. *Jesus, give me your holiness. I ask you for your holiness.*

Let us close by receiving the benediction Paul pronounces at the end of his first letter to the Thessalonians. I offer it as a benediction to you:

> May God himself, the God of peace, sanctify you through and through. May your whole spirit and soul and body be kept blameless at the coming of our Lord Jesus Christ. The one who calls you is faithful and he will do it. (1 Thessalonians 5:23)

Amen.

A CLOSING WORD FROM THE AUTHOR

There is so much more to be said. I hope that you have found this book helpful. I hope that it has brought healing, wholeness, and new fields of goodness to your heart and mind and life. If you enjoyed this, there's more. Lots more. We have all kinds of additional recordings, teachings, books, live events, and resources on our website: www.ransomedheart.com. Come and be refreshed!

But let me also recommend some authors I return to again and again when it comes to questions of holiness and wholeness. I love A. W. Tozer; my favorite book of his is *The Pursuit of God*. If you want to read more on healing, I recommend Leanne Payne's *The Healing Presence*, on inviting the healing work of Christ in your life. And one of my all-time favorites is by nineteenth-century Scot George MacDonald, pastor, theologian, author, and poet. His book *Unspoken Sermons,* while difficult to find, is an incredible work on holiness and living a life of goodness. I think you'll find his understanding of the Gospel refreshing.

There is a way to be good again.

John

THE "DAILY PRAYER"

My dear Lord Jesus, I come to you now to be restored in you, to be renewed in you, to receive from you all the grace and mercy I so desperately need this day. I honor you as my sovereign Lord, and I surrender every aspect of my life totally and completely to you. I give you my spirit, soul and body, my heart, mind and will. Cover me with your blood—my spirit, soul and body, my heart, mind and will. I ask your Holy Spirit to restore me in you, renew me in you, and lead this time of prayer.

[For husbands and/or parents] In all that I now pray, I include [my wife, and/or my children, by name]. Acting as their head, I bring them under your authority and covering. May the blood of Christ cover their spirit, soul and body, their heart, mind and will. Holy Spirit restore them in you, renew them in you and include them in this time of prayer.

Dearest God, holy and victorious Trinity, you alone are worthy of all my worship, my heart's devotion, all my praise and all my trust and all the glory of my life. I love you, I worship you, and I give myself over to you in my heart's search for life. You alone are Life, and you have become my life. I renounce all other gods, every idol, and I give you God the place in my heart and in my life that you truly deserve. I confess here and now that it is all about you, God, and not about me. You are the Hero of this story, and I belong to you. I ask your forgiveness for my every sin. Search me and know me and reveal to me where you are working in my life and grant me your healing, deliverance and the grace of a deep and true repentance.

Heavenly Father, thank you for loving me and choosing me before you made the world. You are my true Father—my creator, redeemer, sustainer, and the true end of all things, including my life. I love you, I worship you, I trust you. I give myself over to you to be one with you as Jesus is one with you. Father, thank you for sending Jesus. I receive him, and all his life and all his work that you provided for me. Thank you for including me in Christ, for forgiving me my sins, granting me his righteousness, for making me complete in him. Thank you for making me alive with Christ, raising me with him, seating me with him at your right hand, establishing me in his authority and anointing me with your Spirit and your love. I receive it with thanks, and I give it total claim to my spirit, soul and body, my heart, mind and will.

Jesus, thank you for coming to ransom me with your own life. I love you, I worship you, I trust you. I give myself over to you now to be one with you in all things. I sincerely receive all the work and triumph of your cross, death, blood and sacrifice for me, through which my every sin is atoned for, I am ransomed and delivered from the kingdom of darkness, my sin nature is removed, my heart is circumcised unto God, and every claim being made against me is disarmed. I now take my place in your cross and death this morning, dying with you to sin, to my flesh, to this world, and to the evil one and his kingdom. I take up the cross and crucify my flesh with all its pride, arrogance, unbelief, and idolatry; I crucify the self-life, all self-saving and self-securing. I put off the old man. I ask you God to apply to me the fullness of the cross, death, blood and sacrifice of Jesus Christ. I receive it with thanks and give it total claim to my spirit, soul and body, my heart, mind and will.

Jesus, I also sincerely receive you as my life, my holiness, and I receive all the work and triumph of your resurrection, through which you have conquered sin, death and judgment. Death has no mastery over you and I have been raised with you to a new life, to live your life—dead to sin and alive to God. I now take my place in your resurrection and in your life, through which I am saved by your life, I reign in life through your life. I give my life to you today to live your life. I receive your joy, love, hope and faith; your union with our Father; your wisdom, understanding and discernment; your courage and power; your holiness, integrity and trueness in all things. I put on the new man. I ask you God to apply to me the fullness of the life and resurrection of Jesus Christ. I receive it with thanks and give it total claim to my spirit, soul and body, my heart, mind and will.

Jesus, I also sincerely receive you as my authority, rule, and dominion, my everlasting victory against Satan and his kingdom, and my authority to bring your Kingdom at all times and

in every way. I receive all the work and triumph of your As-
cension, whereby Satan is judged and cast down, all authority
in heaven and on earth has been given to you, and I have been
given fullness in you, in your authority and in your throne.
I take my place now in your authority and in your throne,
whereby I have been raised with you to the right hand of the
Father and established in your authority. I give my life to you to
reign with you. I now bring the authority, rule and dominion of
the Lord Jesus Christ over my life today—over my spirit, soul
and body, over my heart, mind and will. I bring the authority
of Christ over my home and family and all my kingdom and
domain.

Holy Spirit, thank you for coming. I love you, I worship you,
I trust you. I sincerely receive you and I receive all the work and
victory in Pentecost, whereby you have come, you have clothed
me with power from on high, sealed me in Christ, you have be-
come my union with the Father and the Son, become the Spirit
of truth in me, the life of God in me, my Counselor, Comforter,
Strength, and Guide. I honor you as my sovereign, and I fully
give to you now every aspect and dimension of my life—my
spirit, soul and body, my heart, mind and will—to be filled with
you, to walk in step with you in all things. Fill me afresh. Re-
store my union with the Father and the Son. Lead me into all
truth, anoint me for all of my life and walk and calling, and lead
me deeper into Jesus today. I receive you with thanks, and I give
you total claim to my life.

Heavenly Father, thank you for granting to me every spiritual blessing in Christ Jesus. I claim the riches in Christ Jesus over my life today, over my [wife and children by name], my home and all my domain. I bring the blood of Christ once more over my spirit, soul, and body, my heart, mind and will [over wife and/or children by name, their spirit, soul, and body, heart, mind and will]. Armor me with your armor. I put on the belt of truth, breastplate of righteousness, shoes of the gospel, helmet of salvation. I take up the shield of faith and sword of the Spirit, and I choose to wield these weapons at all times in the power of God. I choose to pray at all times in the Spirit.

Thank you for your angels. I summon them now in the name of the Lord Jesus Christ and instruct them to establish your Kingdom over me and throughout my kingdom and domain, to minister to me your ministry, and to be my companions in the way this day. I now call forth the kingdom of the Lord Jesus Christ throughout my home, my family, my household, my kingdom in the authority of the Lord Jesus Christ, and in his Name, with all glory and honor and thanks to him.

Do you wish this wasn't the end?
Are you hungry for more great teaching, inspiring
testimonies, ideas to challenge your faith?

Join us at www.hodderfaith.com, follow us on Twitter
or find us on Facebook to make sure you get the latest from
your favourite authors.

Including interviews, videos, articles, competitions
and opportunities to tell us just what you thought about
our latest releases.

www.hodderfaith.com

 HodderFaith

 @HodderFaith

 HodderFaithVideo

HODDER
WHERE FAITH IS INSPIRED